In a Blink

Why We Must Be Ready for the Rapture

Kevin Turnbaugh

RIVER BIRCH PRESS

Daphne, Alabama

ISBN 978-1-956365-31-3 (print)
ISBN 978-1-956365-32-0 (e-book)

For Worldwide Distribution
Printed in the U.S.A.

River Birch Press
P.O. Box 868, Daphne, AL 36526

Contents

This book is dedicated to you, the reader, especially those of you who have never asked Jesus Christ to be your Savior. Whether you have not seen the need to do so at this time, have never heard the message of His sacrifice for your sins, or you just do not believe in God. This book has been written from my heart to you, and my desire is that you will accept Jesus as Lord and Savior; and that I may meet and spend eternity in heaven with you and many others.

My goal in writing of all my books is this: so even just one person will walk up to me in heaven and tell me that what they read in my book is the reason they are in heaven. I pray that person will be you!

1

Introduction

On August 18, 1984, my day started out normal enough. I kissed my wife, Lori, goodbye and left for my workday at the shoe factory where I was employed as an industrial engineer and assisted in the design of new shoe patterns from a cost and manufacturing view. After that day, I had an eye exam appointment with a new doctor, as I was experiencing some difficulties that made me think I needed to go back to wearing glasses.

It seemed that as I would walk through the office, and in areas of the manufacturing building, I would hit or bump into objects and/or people. I could not understand why this was happening; it was just as if they were not there. Plus, it had been a couple of years since my original doctor had retired, and an eye exam by a doctor at an eyeglass chain store told me that I did not need glasses. I had worn bifocal glasses since fourth grade, and I should have been skeptical of his diagnosis. My ignorance of this part of my health showed its ugly head that day.

I had been driving since I was sixteen, and that freedom of movement was one of my most cherished pleasures in life. I had been recommended to this new doctor by a coworker in the office whose daughter's eye problems were diagnosed at an early age by this doctor. I arrived at my appointment fully expecting to need to return to wearing glasses.

The exam started out normal enough, but it turned very disturbing quite quickly. The doctor took me into a specially equipped room, ran some eye view and reactionary tests, and gave out a heavy sigh. I figured it had been a long day for him too, so my first reaction was no reaction at all. But he sat back and told me "Kevin, I believe you may have an eye disease called retinitis pigmentosa." My mind went immediately back to a television ad I had seen previously, where the then current professional football player described some of the symptoms of this disease commonly referred to as RP. I remember telling myself, *That sounds like me.* However, I just dismissed the symptoms as coincidental.

The doctor's diagnosis did not hit me too hard until he mentioned that it was an incurable disease that would result in some measure of blindness. Bam! Blindness? I was in immediate denial, but before I could say a thing, he said that he was going to send me to Johns Hopkins' Wilmer Eye Institute in Baltimore, Maryland, to have his diagnosis verified. Before I left his office, the office staff had an appointment for me at Johns Hopkins (JH) for that following October, and out the door I went in a daze and total disbelief.

The drive home was difficult, trying to move through traffic with tears in my eyes. I was also trying to figure out how I was going to tell Lori, who had been my wife for only one year and two months. What had started out as a regular day was now anything but normal!

Our first home was a mobile home in Abbottstown, Pennsylvania, which I had purchased a few years earlier. It had been a great bachelor's pad. As I drove up the street to our home, I almost turned around, having no idea how to tell Lori, or what her reaction would be to such devastating news.

Crazy thoughts about how I would ever be able to drive again, play tennis with friends, mow the lawn, and so on rushed into my head. I saw myself on a street corner trying to sell pencils from a tin cup and just did not see any hope in my future. I must admit, I gave little thought to God at this time or His plans for my situation.

I remember walking into our home, greeting my beautiful wife, and trying to hide that I had been crying. Yeah, I tried to do that "men don't cry" thing, but I was not able to do it for very long. Lori was working on what to make for supper when I asked her to sit down with me a minute. At that moment, our dear cocker spaniel, Cricket, came to greet me, and the tears started to flow.

I began to describe the steps of what happened at the eye doctor's office, and Lori knew something was not right. When I gave her the news of his diagnosis of RP and that I was going to JH, I was scared how I had presented it and how she would respond. I remember saying, "Please do not leave me," and Lori assured me she would not. As of this writing, we just celebrated our thirty-eighth anniversary, and I thank the Lord for Lori standing by me all these years.

Between the time of that very bad day and the time I would go to JH, I held onto a very thin hope that the doctor's diagnosis would be wrong. I shared the results of the doctor's exam at church and my workplace, and with friends and family, especially with my parents, who were living in Texas at the time. The prayers went up, and I did some deep soul-searching and made some things right with God that were out of place at that time.

3

As I waited for that day at JH, I took more notice of what I could and could not see, and it became quite evident that there was an area the size of a donut in which I was unable to notice any movement or identify objects or people.

The trip to JH was not far from where we lived, as we were around ten miles from the Maryland border, and it took only about two hours to get there. If you have never been to JH, or any other university medical center, they are very large, something kids say today is "ginormous." Johns Hopkins fits that description, taking up several city blocks in Baltimore. It was challenging finding our way to the location of my appointment; thank goodness they had an information desk there that directed us to where we needed to go.

The appointment started with a raft of eye examinations, including visual fields test that documented what I could and could not see, a color identification test, and an Electroretinogram (ERG) that required the placing of special contacts connected to the machine onto my eyes. After several hours of testing and my eyes dilated at least twice, I met with the lead ophthalmologist for RP research at that time, who gave me the bad news that the RP diagnosis had been confirmed by the tests.

The drive home was every bit as bad as the drive from the eye doctor in August. Only this time there was no doubt of the diagnosis, just what the future had to hold for Lori and me. Part of my visit to JH was to investigate any eye history on my parents' ancestry. This is what is called a genealogy study, and the results would determine future actions and appointments at JH.

After we shared the results with my parents, they dove into their respective family histories. However, we knew this would be a challenge on my mother's side, as she was adopted at a young age. My dad's history showed nothing more than regular corrections with glasses, but we were told that our family history included a Union Civil War hero at the battle of Gettysburg, a fact we have not been able to verify.

However, my mother's family history revealed some bad news. Although she was adopted young, Mom kept in contact with one biological sister living in Indiana. She revealed that my biological grandfather was blind, a fact my mom and aunt had already known, and his blindness had been attributed to being exposed to the gases used during World War I, of which he was a veteran. But Mom's sister revealed that her son was also a victim of RP, and evidence came together that their dad must have also suffered from RP, the girls were carriers, and their sons became victims of RP as well. The medical term for this is an X-linked dominant inheritance.

After this information had been uncovered, Mom was blaming herself for ruining my life, and Dad and I had quite a time getting her settled down over the next several months. We participated in a study at JH and a DNA tracking study with the University of Michigan, but the evidence of how RP became a part of my future was very evident.

A well-known cliché says that everything has a silver lining in it somewhere, and my diagnosis of RP was no exception. At the end of my initial visit to JH, I was given several research documents about the eye from numerous universities, and not all about RP specifically. Over the next several weeks, I read with great intensity all the documents, absorbed the information as best I could, and shared it with Lori. Then at my next visit to my family doctor, I gave the documents to him for the same reason JH had given them to me.

One of these research papers made a great impression on me and was one of the main reasons for my first book titled *Time Witnessing*, and in a greater way, the very foundation of this book.

I first taught my study called Time Witnessing when I was asked to substitute teach my Sunday School class at church. The Lord laid upon me this paper, its contents, how it could be related to my diagnosis, and how it relates to what the apostle Paul wrote in 1 Corinthians 15 and 1 Thessalonians 4 and 5.

Let's see how this research paper and God's Word helps us to understand why we must be ready for the rapture of the Christians, and what "in a twinkling of an eye" really means. When we look at the recent events of just the last few years and decades, the reasons and evidence of the imminent return of Jesus Christ for His bride could not be clearer.

2

The Miracle of the Eye

According to the online concordance *Bible Gateway*, the word "eye" is mentioned in the Bible 571 times. In 1905 Civilla D. Martin wrote the words to the song "His Eye Is on the Sparrow," and Charles H. Gabriel composed it. The Bible says that when God created humans, He created us in His own image (Genesis 1:26-27). In God's creation of all things, He made all things perfect. However, when Adam and Eve sinned by following the temptation of Satan in the form of the serpent, God's creation was no longer perfect due to sin in the world (Genesis 3).

I often hear people expressing a desire to know where all the evil, savagery, hate, diseases, and adverse weather comes from. They need not look any further than Satan's temptation of Adam and Eve and all the wrongs that sinful decision caused. In Genesis 6-9, we learn that sin became so evil over the centuries that except for those on the ark during the flood, God destroyed every living thing.

What does sin have to do with the eye? Among those things that sin allowed to enter the world were some of those physical ailments many of us experience over our lifetimes. Yes, we have found cures for disastrous afflictions like bubonic plague (also known as the Black Death) and smallpox, but no one to date has been able to cure the pesty common cold.

In all God's creation, except for plant life, all creatures have eyes. Some fish do not and live in darkness, and bats are for the most part blind and depend on a very sophisticated sonar system with their ears to fly and locate insects. Snakes do have eyes but depend on sensors in their tongue to guide them to their prey. Then some insects have numerous eyes in a cluster by which they move and fly.

The position of eyes on creatures differs as well. Humans, dogs, cats, bears, etc. have our eyes looking forward. Animals like horses, zebras, and the like have their eyes on the sides of their heads; this is the same for most birds. The eyes of the chameleon lizard are mounted on each side; however, it can move them in many directions individually for its security and in locating food.

Through our eyes we identify people or objects, see dangers and avoid them, drive cars or horses, and many other functions. During my time in the shoe factory, I would observe the workers as they performed their part in making the shoes, some of which were quite technical and required a well-focused vision of the task. Our eyes allow us to enjoy the magnificent colors of the trees in autumn or of paintings, or even the colors of Hawaii's state fish, a very colorful triggerfish, called an Hawaiian Humuhumunukunukuapuaa (meaning triggerfish with a pig snout). Don't worry, I cannot pronounce it either.

Of the five senses we have—sight, hearing, feel, taste, and smell—our eyes are the only one of them directly attached to our brain. They are the most detailed cameras ever created, with several components that obtain and project the world onto a layer of "film" we call the retina. The retina is a very delicate, ultra-thin group of photosensitive cells. The world is then sent directly to the brain, via our optic nerve from each eye, to an area at the back of the brain. This area is in the very back of our skull, where we feel a small notch at the base of the skull.

Those of you who must wear glasses to provide yourself "perfect" vision, might be wondering at this point if God's creation was so perfect, what's up with my eyes as they are in my body? All of the imperfections in this world can be directed back to that meeting between Satan in the form of the serpent, and Adam and Eve. Since that time, all of those things that are less than perfect have existed.

There are many reasons for less than perfect 20/20 vision. Some of us are nearsighted, some are farsighted, and the list of correctable imperfections goes on. But there several imperfections that are not correctable. One that is so sad is when one is born blind. Another is the development of glaucoma, which leads to irreversible blindness. Still another is eye cancer. When we are younger, these difficulties can be quite devastating, but they are not so easy when one is older either, as I can well attest. Even older adults can develop macular degeneration problems located behind the eye, at the optic nerve connection.

Now I am not an ophthalmologist, optician, or medically trained in matters of the eye; however, one does learn quite a bit from being a victim of one of these diseases and ailments of the eye. In my initial visit to JH, I learned more biological information about the eye than I ever had known before, including the components of the eye and their functions.

In addition, I learned how the rest of my senses, except taste, would become so much more important than they had ever been before. My hearing, sense of feel and yes, even smell would help me to maneuver when using a white cane. These same senses would be part of learning to walk with a guide dog.

Seeing and hearing are the two senses we use to become educated in school. So, knowing something about these parts of our person and protecting them from outside sources of harm can and should be right up there at the top of our list of taking care of ourselves. One does not want to stare at the sun or anything like a very bright light. The same is true with our hearing. I have a problem at concerts when the band cranks up the sound, and you see the performers wearing hearing protection during the show.

The eyes are not the strongest components of the body either. If you have ever poked yourself in the eye, you know this fact quite well. I remember seeing the old Three Stooges shorts and laughing so hard as Moe poked Curly in the eyes. However, what they did, we must avoid doing to prevent possible permanent damage to the eyes.

You might be wondering how the senses of taste, touch, and smell could be helpful to a person who is visually handicapped or totally blind. When I was first diagnosed with RP, I soon started to learn how to get around with the aid of a white cane. Here feeling is very important, as the cane can and will tell the person so many things and even keep us from dangers.

In today's training of visually challenged persons, tapping the cane left and right is no longer used. Instead, canes are equipped with one of several types of roller tips so the cane can be swung left to right. In this way the user can feel cracks in the sidewalk, not miss an obstacle that is directly in front of them, and have a much better knowledge of conditions in front of them. With the cane, touch becomes so much more important.

Hearing is just as much important. Trainers will instruct the user to listen to what is around them. Sounds like a playground where children are playing and laughing can and will orientate the person as to where they are on their walk. How to stop at an intersection, listening to how the cars come, stop, and go will help the user to determine if they are at a two-way stop, four-way stop, or an intersection operated by a stoplight system.

The use of smell also helps a person determine their location, whether they are nearing an intersection, etc. A particular restaurant's unique smell, like Oriental or Mexican foods, tell us where we are in certain areas.

Putting all these other senses to work, whether walking with a cane or a trained guide dog, assists the blind to have a measure of freedom. Also, in today's world, the sight of a white cane or correctly harnessed guide dog can be a signal to others to make space for us to proceed on our walk.

Many abnormalities affect the eyes. Cataracts may form on the lens and can be corrected today by having man-made lenses put in their place. The iris controls the amount of light, or lack thereof, that is allowed to enter the eyes. However, an incorrectly functioning iris could prevent a person from tolerating sunshine very well without very dark sunglasses. Problems within the eyeball itself and failures of the rods in that area will cause different types of visual difficulties.

The problem I am so very much familiar with in the eye is the eye disease I described in the introduction. The disease RP is a type of matter that covers the retina, preventing the photosensitive cells of the retina from receiving that which passes through the lens, iris, etc. Although you can look up the technical details of RP, I describe it as what you get if you expose the old type of film you had in a camera. The picture may have been taken, but all you got was a fuzzy and blank photo. If you younger folks have no clue what film is, take your iPhone, point it at a blank white wall, take a picture, and look at what you get.

Older folks can develop a disease called macular degeneration, which forms behind the eyeball and disrupts the interaction with the optic nerve. This disease and RP are closely related medically and causes the same kind of sight prevention.

Finally, the optic nerve is the physical avenue by which the brain receives the view from the eyes and what registers in our brain as the trees, people, etc. we see. Any damage to this nerve can and usually does result in permanent blindness.

Other areas around the eyes are in place for the protection and even care of the eyes. The eyebrows, eyelashes, eyelids— and even the fact the eyes are located within recessed sockets— all contribute to protecting these vital organs of our amazing bodies created in the image of our God.

3

Warnings of Future Times

Ever since time began and sin entered the lives of humans, we have had this idea that what another person says, has, does, the language they speak, etc., are reasons to inflict onto them our will, feelings, and desires. The first battle between us was that between Cain and Abel (Genesis 4), and we have not stopped since. After God confused the languages of the people at Nimrod's building of the Tower of Babble (Genesis 10 and 11), the world has not been the same since.

Moses recorded in Exodus the military capabilities of the ancient Egyptians, with all of Pharaoh's chariots and other battle equipment. As the centuries passed, peoples and nations gave more importance to their war abilities and equipment developments than they did to feeding their own populations.

Some wars were justified, like the Revolutionary War, that gave the thirteen colonies their independence from the tyrannical rule of England and its religious rules dictated by the king at that time. Not so justified was America's Civil War, where the Confederate States fought to retain their right to slavery and cost thousands of American lives at the hand of their own countrymen.

We cannot seem to survive as humans without researching, developing, testing, and improving our abilities to inflict more severe harm upon each other. In fact, this area of business in the world has sales into the hundreds of billions of dollars annually. This fact was prophesied in the Bible by numerous book authors, writing under the authority and inspiration of God Almighty. Included in these prophesies was those words recorded by Jesus Christ Himself.

Both history and the Bible record numerous conflicts between nations, people, followers of one false god against someone else's false god, or against followers of God Almighty. First, battles were on land only, then warships made for battles on the water. Since the Wright brothers' invention in 1903, we added combat in the air; we have also added war under water too.

Do we learn from history? No! We justify our actions to ourselves, and after a while come out swinging, just like a boxer who does not know when to quit. They have it and we want it. I am not the center of attention, so I will get some attention by attacking someone. Over the centuries, the senseless reasons for starting wars have been numerous, ever since that brotherly conflict between Cain and Abel.

A similar type of greed was most apparent from those dictatorial leaders of Germany, Italy, and Japan, and that led to WWII. Hitler and Mussolini's cause were simply a land grab; however, Emperor Hirohito's cause was to obtain lands to help Japan with raw materials and oil.

In the later years of the 1930s, the signs of war on the horizon became more and more apparent from the actions of these tyrannical leaders. In Matthew 24, Jesus gives us signs of the coming end times, as recorded by Matthew, who was one of Jesus' disciples. In addition, the apostle Paul also gives us signs and warnings why we need to be ready for these coming end times.

Just as many ignored the signs of the coming WWII, we

cannot ignore what is coming, which will lead to the end of all things as we know them to be today. These prophesied end times are the reasons why Christians should pursue fulfilling Jesus' command to be witnesses for Him (Acts 1:8). It also had everything to do with the name of my first book, *Time Witnessing*.

As we continue through this book, take special notice of the prophesied coming end times signs and look at those events in our world today. So many of these signs are being passed off as Mother Nature rearing her ugly head. Others shrug it off, especially people who see the devastation from an earthquake, tornado, or hurricane, are thankful it was not them, and go about their business without another thought.

Years ago, a painter demonstrated this denial and ignoring of events, and how people dealt with what was going on around them: with three monkeys sitting next to each other. One had his hands over the eyes, the second over his ears, and the third over his mouth. It was titled "See no evil, hear no evil, and speak no evil." This reaction is exactly how people today are treating events in the world, figuring they will just go away and wanting to move on to the next subject.

Being ready for the coming end times begins with one being a follower of Jesus Christ. In John 3, Jesus described to Nicodemus, and to us today, that we must accept Him (Jesus) as our personal Savior. This is a spiritual rebirth and will change our inner person and make each of us a child of God. It also guarantees us a place in heaven and prepares us for that day when He will rapture us from the Earth.

We will look deep into this being ready, and the signs that tell us to always be ready, in the coming chapters.

However, I want to know if you can remember a day when

you asked Jesus into your heart? If not, now (not at the end of the book) is the time to do this, as I cannot guarantee if I will finish this book before the rapture occurs. You see, the Bible does not tell us when it will occur, it just gives us signs of its coming. Please pray that prayer now, or you will be left behind.

4

Prophesied Signs

Read: Ezekiel 37 and the book of Daniel

In the world today, just about everything is directed by the use of signs. While driving, signs tell us what the next road or route number is, and cities have street name signs, stop signs, etc. In other countries, instead of words they utilize symbols, like a left turn arrow with a red circle and a slash across it means no left turns at that intersection.

Other signs advise us of gas stations and/or restaurants coming up at the next exit. Still others warn us of equipment that is not working. Some restaurant entrances instruct us that "no shirt, no shoes, no service." All these signs are in the places they are to inform us, direct us, or warn us to avoid potential dangers.

In the Bible we have signs too, put there to instruct us in living our lives according to God's desire and will. Also included are the warning signs of those events to come that alert us of the coming end times. Both the Old and New Testaments contain these signs.

Some of these signs are found in several books and others in just a few or only one. For example, Joel refers to the "blood moon" during the tribulation period (Joel 2:31), and this event is also recorded in Acts 2:20 and Revelation 6:12.

17

During my dad's forty-five years in the ministry, he wore out a particular classic pastor's comment. It refers to Scripture verses that begin with the word "therefore." The saying goes that we need to know and learn what it is there for, and on goes the message. There are no exceptions for the signs of the coming end times, as we need to know and heed them, and learn what they are there for too.

If we did a detailed study on all the signs in the Bible, that would result in a book of its own. However, in this chapter we are going to look at a vision of the prophet Ezekiel, followed by a dream interpreted by Daniel, and then a dream that the angel Gabriel delivered to Daniel.

In Ezekiel 37, the prophet is taken to a valley full of old dried-up human bones. Now Ezekiel was one of God's prophets during the time that most of the Jews from the northern and southern kingdoms of Israel had been taken into captivity by King Nebuchadnezzar and the Babylonians. On behalf of the Jews, Ezekiel asked for a sign from God on the future of the Jews. He was asking for himself as well as the rest of the Jewish captives because Ezekiel and other prophets before him knew that the Jews had sinned before God with their worship of idols.

We learn in the book of Daniel that the Jews would be kept in captivity for a period of seventy years. Also, Ezekiel's vision would not concern the Jews' return as described in the books of Ezra and Nehemiah. Instead, this vision was of a return that would not occur until our modern times. Another part of God's vision, and subsequent instructions to Ezekiel, involved how the Jews would come back to the Promised Land, what we call the Holy Land or Israel today.

What Ezekiel saw in his vision was a valley covered in bones. God asked him if these bones could live again, and Ezekiel's response was that only God knew that answer. In a two-step instruction from God, after Ezekiel spoke to the bones, they all came together and stood up, covered in skin like a great army. Then for the second instruction, Ezekiel spoke to the wind, and it gave breath to those standing before him.

In the latter part of this chapter from Ezekiel, God has the prophet take two sticks, labeled Judah and Israel. He then instructs Ezekiel to form them into one stick, symbolizing that when the Jews did come back into the Holy Land, they would return as a single nation.

This prophecy was fulfilled in May 1948, following WWII. At that time, Israel's first Prime Minister, David Ben Gurion, declared the existence of the "State of Israel."

One of the most important signs of Christ's return for His followers was that the Jews would return to the Holy Land. With the fulfillment of this prophecy, all prophecies for the return of Jesus have been fulfilled.

Then there are the two prominent dream/interpretations we find in the book of Daniel. I referenced the whole book of Daniel because, in addition to the signs we will explore, it is a great guide to all of us on how we should live our everyday lives before God.

The books of Ezekiel and Daniel intertwine, as they cover the same timeframe. Both were written during or near the Jews' captivity in Babylon under tyrannical King Nebuchadnezzar. One provides a prophecy of hope for the future of the Jews; the other is an understanding of events that have already occurred (as of this writing) and are to come. None of the Jews of that time would see them come to pass; however, their future descendants would, and we can hold on to these prophecies today too.

Daniel, who the king renamed Belteshazzar, and his three fellow young Jews: Hananiah renamed Shadrach, Mishael renamed Meshach, and Azariah renamed Abed-Nego were all taken into captivity as teenagers, never to see their Jewish homeland again. However, they held true to the Mosaic law and refused to eat the food provided to them by the king because it had been brought to them after being offered to the false gods of the Babylonians. God would honor these men for this act and for their refusal to worship the idol set up by the king.

King Nebuchadnezzar had a dream, and he wanted it interpreted. He called all his wise men, insisted they tell him his dream, and demanded they interpret it. They could not fulfill the king's demand, and he ordered that they all be put to death. However, Daniel requested to be allowed to provide the interpretation. After God provided Daniel with the dream and its interpretation, he came before the king with the dream and its meaning.

Daniel told the king that he had dreamed of a very large image of a man. The image had a head of gold representing the Babylonian kingdom. The remaining parts represented the kingdoms that would succeed Babylon. Today, we know that the silver represented the Medes-Persians, the bronze the Greeks under Alexander the Great, and the legs of iron the Roman Empire that eventually split into two halves.

What was interpreted for the king is also part of the signs of what is to come, as the feet made of iron and clay pertain to the reign of the Antichrist during the tribulation, with the ten toes of clay the ten kingdoms under him. This part of the image is yet to come, but then the dream ended with a great stone destroying the image. The stone is a metaphorical representation of when Jesus will return at the end of the seven-year tribulation period and will be King over all, destroying the reign of the Antichrist. It would be the second vision of Daniel, recorded in the later part of his book, sharing why we must be ready for that day when the rapture will occur.

Beginning in chapter 7, Daniel had two very similar visions. Both consisted of creatures rising with what were metaphorical descriptions. The first two creatures seen by Daniel represented the kingdoms like the gold and silver parts of King Nebuchadnezzar saw in his dream.

The third beast, with four heads and the like, represented the bronze kingdom that Alexander the Great had conquered; but after his death, it would be split into four parts, each headed by one of his subordinate generals.

It was the fourth beast that represented the same as the feet and toes of the image dreamed by the king. The ten horns were the ten kingdoms that will be under the Antichrist during the tribulation period, and the little horn in the middle that spoke blasphemous words represented the Antichrist himself.

These prominent signs/prophecies from the Old Testament are signs for us today as well. Just as the prophecy of Ezekiel that described the return of the Jews to the Holy Land was fulfilled in May 1948, we can know that what was described in Daniel will come to be in the future too. However, by accepting Jesus as your Savior, you can avoid the last part of these dreams and visions. If you have not done so before, now would be a great time to do so to be guaranteed eternity in heaven.

5

Jesus, Savior, and Deliverer

Read: John 1

During the horrors of WWII, several examples can be found of how Allied forces rescued or saved soldiers captured or facing imminent danger. One was of captives in a Japanese prisoner-of-war camp when they saw hundreds of parachutes that resulted in their being freed from the horrible conditions under their Japanese captors. My great-aunt Elda Amstutz, a missionary to India during this time, had the boat she and fellow missionaries were sailing to India captured by the Japanese, and they were held for a large part of the war.

Another example is the surrounded garrison of American soldiers at the city of Batstone in Belgium. When given an ultimatum by the attacking Germans during the Battle of the Bulge, the commander replied with a single word reply of "Nuts." Shortly after that reply, American forces under the command of Lieutenant General George S. Patton entered the area, pushed back the Germans, and rescued the survivors from certain death or imprisonment.

The apostle John begins his Gospel with a description of who exactly Jesus was and is "the Word" (John 1:1). Later, John the Baptist introduced Jesus to those gathered around him,

"Behold the Lamb of God" (John 1:29). In the famous John 3:16 verse, we are told that God loved His creation so much that He sent His Son Jesus to pay the price for the sins of the world.

What the people of the world have not understood, choose not to believe, or are prevented from hearing and learning, is that the payment for all our sins was paid for on that cruel Roman cross, on the day we know as Good Friday.

However, many reject the salvation provided to us on that day, and the guarantee of eternity in heaven, due to Jesus' resurrection from the dead on the day we know as Easter Sunday. This sacrifice of God's only Son was necessary, as no other could fulfill the requirement for the payment for sin.

When this salvation is but a prayer of acceptance, why do so many reject it? The simple answer is unbelief caused by Satan's influence. I have been on the receiving end of blasts from atheists, who just do not believe in a supreme being they often call the "flying spaghetti monster." Others are prevented from even hearing about Jesus because it would take away from their firm control of their population. Then there are those so-called religions that are nothing short of cults, led by leaders possessed by Satan and his demons.

Evidence of Satan's influence upon one of these religions can be seen in their holy day of prayer on Fridays. They pray to their god, whose name is just another reference to Satan. If any of their followers drift away, they will be put to death. Even speaking out against their religion can result in a death sentence, as Sir Salman Rushdie, who authored the book *The Satanic Verses,* can well attest.

It is from Jesus' death and resurrection that He is our Savior, and only by asking for one's forgiveness of sins and accepting Jesus as our Savior can one guarantee their future in heaven. Jesus is also our deliverer as well—not just from eternity in hell, but also from having to endure the seven years of the tribulation period.

In addition to the prophesies and visions in Ezekiel and Daniel noted previously, Jesus Himself gave us some significant signs of the coming end times. He also demonstrated to His disciples and those who followed Him, like the Gospel writer Luke (who also wrote the book of Acts), how to handle actions taken toward the followers of the one and only true God.

All through the Gospel books of Matthew, Mark, Luke, and John, Jesus is being challenged by the head of the Jewish people, known as the Sanhedrin, and its components called the Pharisees. The Sadducees and scribes added to the challenges of Jesus' authority.

I must admit to my being humored by how Jesus really put these so-called religious leaders in their place so often in the Gospels. As I have stated on many occasions before, what really irritated these folks was that Jesus rained on their parade. They just adored the attention they received from the people to the point that they desired it more than overseeing the enforcement of the Mosaic law. Then when Jesus would cross the line, in their opinion, they would rush in and challenge Him in front of the people, only to be humbled and humiliated.

Jesus also taught and demonstrated that we should not tolerate what is not acceptable in God's sight. He made this quite clear when He made a whip and chased the money changers from the temple (Matthew 21:12; Mark 11:15; John 2:14-15). This is the reason why we Christians will not give any tolerance to any sinful actions.

I have been criticized on several occasions from Christians and non-Christians alike about my fierce opposition to the LGBTQ+ movement and the mindless abortion of babies. I am also very outspoken about the courts ordering the removal of crosses, Christian flags, Ten Commandments plaques and monuments, and nativity scenes and anything associated with Christmas from public view.

In the Bible, Christians are encouraged to be meek, not weak, in our dealings with others (Psalms 37:11; Matthew 5:5). When we see or hear something that is wrong, we are to speak up and make our displeasures known. If our elected officials do not wish to listen, then speak loudly at the voting booth.

Among those things Jesus made known to His disciples and to us today are signs of His coming to rapture us prior to the tribulation period. In the next few chapters, we are going to look at these signs in detail and how they are so relevant to what we are experiencing today.

The most important point He made was the timing is not known, even to Jesus Himself. In Matthew 24:36-37, He clearly makes it known that the day and time of His return for Christians is known only by God the Father. However, we are provided with signs of this coming event; and it is these signs we will look at next.

Although we do not know the date of His return, it is not a reason to put off your accepting Jesus as Savior. That day could be today, and the very moment you are reading these words, put down the book, and ask Him to be your Savior right now. You will be eternally grateful you did!

6

Signs of Jesus' Return

Read: Matthew 24

Having been the son of a minister, I picked up some of the "business" words of the profession. However, you need not worry about my use of big ministry words known as homiletics. I not only do not know what they mean, I needed help from my spell checker to even spell the word. But one thing I did learn is what is known as an expository study of a portion of Scripture, meaning an intense review and understanding of that part of God's Word.

To understand what Jesus told His disciples is a study we must undertake. Please read Matthew 24. Every time I read a part of the Bible referring to the Mount of Olives, my mind goes back to the two occasions I was privileged to visit Israel in the 1970s. In fact, during my second tour, my friends and I actually climbed the mount, walking right through the vast olive tree groves to the summit. So, it is very easy for me to picture Jesus and His disciples overlooking the city of Jerusalem, as Jesus told them of events to come.

In Matthew 24, Jesus tells His disciples that not a single stone (of the temple) would remain in the future. The temple Jesus and His followers were looking at was the one that was built by Herod around 37 BCE, as the first temple built under

King Solomon had been destroyed by the invading Babylonians (2 Kings 25:1-21).

This first sign spoken by Jesus was realized when the Romans, under the command of their General Titus, destroyed Herod's temple in 79 CE. Along with this destruction, the Jewish nation was no more, and the Jews were scattered throughout the known world, much in the same way as the dry bones in Ezekiel's vision.

At this point of Jesus' ministry on Earth, the disciples were like many others, wondering when Jesus, the promised Messiah, would remove the Roman occupiers and establish His kingdom. What they had not fully grasped was the real reason Jesus had come to Earth. They were looking for freedom from Rome, but Jesus had come to provide freedom from their sins. In addition, they willingly followed Jesus but did not fully understand His deity, abilities to heal, and the basis of His ministry.

The Bible does not give us information about the disciples after the book of Acts. We do know that James, the brother of John, was beheaded for his service, and John was exiled to the island of Patmos until his death. How the rest met their end is legendary, but if any of the disciples lived or were in Jerusalem when the temple was destroyed is not known.

Matthew is the one disciple recognized as recording the end time signs by Jesus; however, others did record some parts but not in as much detail. I am sure that as the disciples looked upon the temple mount from the Mount of Olives, it had to be hard to imagine how every stone that made up the temple could be removed. Even though they knew full well that Solomon's temple had been destroyed in the past.

This sign, nor the prophecy of Ezekiel, would not be fully

understood until that historical day in May of 1948. Further, the complete fulfillment of Jerusalem in the hands of the Jews would not be realized until after the 1967 Six-Day War. Only after that victory was the sign of the destruction of the temple fully grasped.

Today, only the foundational part of Solomon's temple remains—the Western Wall, also called the Wailing Wall, which was constructed over historical Mount Moriah. On top of this are two mosques, which I call ugly warts, called the Al Aqsa and Dome of the Rock Mosque. To Islam, they make up that religion's third holiest site.

In this area will be found the mount's highest point, and it was at this location known as the pinnacle where Satan tried to tempt Jesus to jump and allow the angels to catch Him (Matthew 4:5-7). Dating back to Abraham and Isaac and their journey recorded in Genesis 22, we are first told of this same Mount Moriah, the summit of which is covered by the Dome of the Rock shrine.

The very fact that not a single stone of the temple will be found at this site today is confirmation of the sign Jesus gave to His disciples. Archeologists are excavating and analyzing the rubble found below the temple mount; however, this is a sign we must recognize as one of the signs of the coming end times.

7

False Christs

When something is stated in the Bible, we should obey. When it is stated twice, we need to take it to heart. However, when it is stated three or more times, we need to take heed and give it the seriousness it deserves. Matthew 24 records of Jesus' warning of those who falsely claim to be Christ, bring forth false teachings, and cause the people to turn away from the truth.

After the Jews left Egypt, Joshua was appointed to lead them into the promised land. One of God's primary commands to the Israelites was to destroy all the men, women, children, and animals in Canaan. The people worshipped idols there, and for that they were to be eliminated completely. One of the main reasons Israel deals with the threats that surround them today comes from Joshua and the Israelites not completely obeying God's command. They started out fine but would be deceived and fail to finish the task.

All through the Old and New Testament of the Bible, we read how the Jews fell in and out of God's favor, switching back and forth between serving God and serving the idols and false gods. This problem continued throughout all the conquerors represented by that image seen in King Nebuchadnezzar's dream. This continued into the Greek and later Roman occupations, with the introduction of the many gods of both Greek and Roman mythology.

However, the warning sign of Jesus was not just concerning the false gods; it was also directed against those who promoted the teachings of following one or more of these gods. He let His disciples know that another sign of His return would be the rise of those who claimed to be the Christ, so they could lead people away from God.

After Jesus' return to heaven in Acts 1, the disciples received the Holy Spirit and began spreading the word of salvation. This movement came to be known as The Way, referring to Jesus' words in John 14:6, where He stated that He was the only way of salvation. Included in this movement was Paul, who had been converted to the cause of Christ on his way to Damascus.

The Jewish leadership were among those who spread false teachings, denying that Jesus was the promised Messiah. This teaching continues to this day by the Orthodox Jews. They were looking for the Messiah to wipe away their occupiers, like the Romans, and because Jesus did not measure up to their expectations, well, Jesus could not have been the Messiah. Since He claimed to be the Son of God, they crucified Him.

During Paul's missionary journeys, he ran up against several false teachings, sorcerers of demonic ways, and the worship of both the Greek and Roman mythical gods. However, he had far more successes throughout his ministry, and today approximately half of the New Testament was written by Paul. Through these books his ministry continues.

All throughout history, false teachers and gods have risen and fallen away, the gods of the ancient Egyptians and Canaanites are lost to history, as well as the gods of the ancient Greeks and Romans. Others have been around for centuries and are no more real than when they first came onto the scene.

Some of these false beliefs even cost humans their lives, in a vane attempt to please or appease these gods. The Old Testament gods of Baal and the Ashtaroth idol were carved out of wood or other types of material; then the people would worship these lifeless things, expecting great wonders and deliverance.

Today, the Hindu religion has hundreds of gods for just about every aspect of life, including the very polluted Ganges River. Ancestors are worshiped in the Shinto religion, and lifeless idols of Buddha are worshiped in many areas of the world. Some of these idols are made out of very costly metals, like the world's largest Buddha idol in Bangkok, Thailand, made out of gold and weighing in at five tons.

Added to the worship of these lifeless idols, there are those that think of themselves as deliverers of utopian life and even claim to be Christ come back to Earth. These cults, led by those who claim to have answers, divine leading, and even the god on Earth, are not "the way." The Pope is referred to as the Holy Father, and priests as Father this or that. But in Matthew 23:9, we are told to refer to no one on Earth as Father, only the Father in heaven. Other popular faiths refer to the head of their movement as prophet.

Some of these cults are dangerous, like the Moonies of the late twentieth century, followers of Scientology, and those who followed the heaven's Gate cult. All those who followed false Christs, such as Jim Jones and David Koresh, paid with their lives. The list of these false, and some very dangerous, cults go on.

These false and cultish followings are all demonic based. Jesus tells us in John 14:6 that He, and only He, is the way of salvation and eternity in heaven. If you find yourself mixed up in one of these false beliefs, run away into the loving arms of Jesus.

8

Conflicts and Threats

In Matthew 24, Mark 13, and Luke 21, the next events pointing to Jesus' return are described as "sorrows." The first of these sorrows are wars and rumors of wars—if we look at history as far back as it has been recorded, these sorrows have been a threat to the people of the Earth from the start. It just seems that we humans cannot get along with anybody. All these conflicts and those threatened in today's world can all be blamed on sin when Adam and Eve brought it into our world.

The only conflict we have record of prior to the flood in Genesis 6-9 is the meeting between Cain and Abel, and how the sin of jealousy cost Abel his life (Genesis 4). However, because the whole Earth had been populated by the time Noah was instructed to build the ark, it would not be hard to imagine that conflicts existed during those prehistoric years.

As we read on in the book of Genesis, conflicts and outright wars seem to have begun following the confusing of the languages in chapters 10 and 11. The people could no longer communicate with each other, fear entered in, and that fear led to one people's fear of another and caused them to feel the only way to resolve their fear was to eliminate the other people. Here again, the sin nature we received from Adam and Eve reared its ugly head.

So many wars in the past can be blamed on one side or the other violating one or more of the Ten Commandments. Those who worship God would be threatened by others who worshiped a false god. Neighborly love was nonexistent between bordering peoples and languages or cultures. Add to that the "they have it and I want it" sinfulness, which violates many of the commandments.

Even in today's world, nations spend more on their military equipment than on feeding their population. One current example is the highly repressive regime of North Korea, officially known as the Democratic People's Republic of Korea (DPRK). This little nation claims a military in excess of one million and has developed nuclear weapon readiness; however, they cannot feed their population, looking for assistance in this area quite often from the world.

Despite this situation, they are constantly rattling their proverbial sabers at South Korea and the rest of the world. What is so sad here is that most of this threatening is to get food contributions and just plain lack of attention toward their leadership.

One ideology many of these nations share is a total and complete rejection of Christianity. Along with North Korea, the nations of China, Nepal, Russia, and others absolutely forbid any Bible teaching or distribution within their borders. However, some successes of God's Word getting into these areas have been realized.

Nation Against Nation

One cannot turn on the television, radio, or other source of news without hearing that this nation is at odds with another nation. Border exchanges occur on a daily basis, or United Nations (UN) Ambassadors are sniping at each other. Then there are the constant threats against Israel from its neighboring countries, a situation that existed ever since Israel was declared a State in May of 1948 and has resulted in several wars that ended in Israel's military prevailing with God Almighty's aid to His cosen people.

History records many wars over the centuries, and some cost thousands of lives. Shamefully, some like the Civil War were fought over whether people had the right to enslave others. At the battle of Gettysburg in 1863, more soldiers were killed in three days than during the entire Vietnam War.

As I am writing this paragraph, Iran and its surrogate nations are threatening to wipe Israel off the world's map, and it continues to enrich uranium for their nuclear abilities. Nuclear equipped China and India are having cross border conflicts; China is creating manmade islands within international waters in the South China Sea, disrupting international commerce in that part of the world.

We are told in the Bible over and over that God is in control, and He is! However, we humans cannot help but fear what may come of these threats, both from external and internal forces. Jesus told us of this sign, but that does not mean we may or may not be directly affected. If the sinful desires of power, dominance, and/or demands toward others exist, these wars and rumors of wars will continue until that day when sin is removed from this world.

9

Human-Caused Disasters

When adverse weather is experienced, it is often said that Mother Nature isn't happy about something. In Hawaii, a volcano on the big island of Hawaii itself has been continuously erupting since 1983; and Hawaiian lore includes the fire goddess named Pele. Earthquakes are blamed on old man Earth, who is showing his age, or something like that kind of comment. But what exactly is the reason for these and other problems like famines occurring from time to time?

Even within the Christian world it is highly debated what the cause of such "natural" occurrences truly is, and why does God allow them to form and come to pass. One of the most difficult things to accept in having faith in God is getting the answer to why. Questions like: why did the tornado have to destroy my home, Lord? Why did the lightning have to hit my barn, Lord? What did I do wrong, Lord, to have had to experience this destruction?

If you have ever experienced one or more of these types of disasters, I do not have the answers. At the beginning of the book of Job, we read of a meeting between God the Father and Lucifer, also known as Satan. God drew attention to Job, and Lucifer challenged how Job would react if he suffered a great loss. God gave Satan free range to do to Job as he wished; however, God told Satan that he could not kill Job. I do not know about you, reader, but I would rather not be the center of discussion between God and Satan. However, Job showed his faithfulness and was restored to health and wealth by God.

One of the reasons Jacob (later named Israel by God) and his vast family moved to Egypt was a severe famine in the land of Canaan. We also read in the book of Ruth that Naomi and her family went to the area called Moab due to a famine in Israel.

History has recorded famines over the centuries. The potato famine in Ireland caused many Irish to immigrate to the US. Even in the 1930s, the middle part of the US experienced famine during a period known as the "dust bowl."

Even with all the modern farming equipment, planting and growing techniques, and agricultural information available, many parts of the world experience some form or measure of famine at times. The very fact that this form of disaster exists is just another sign of these prophesied sorrows and Jesus' soon coming for His own.

The next sign or sorrow listed is that of pestilences. The *Merriam Webster* online dictionary defines pestilence as a "contagious or infectious disease" like the Black Death, small pox, Spanish flu, or even today's Covid 19 pandemic that I call the China virus. No matter what the source or cause, we are experiencing this sorrow (it seems) annually.

Every year people are urged, and some required, to get a flu shot near the beginning of the fall. Despite these actions, thousands will fall victim to the active strain that year, and many will die from the virus. As I am writing this paragraph, the world is experiencing the China virus that has infected millions and has killed nearly four million to date.

In the book of Exodus, God warned Pharaoh, through Moses and Aaron, to let His people the Jews leave and return to the promised land. Pharaoh repeatedly said no, and in response, God sent several kinds of pestilences upon Egypt. The final one cost Pharaoh his first-born son (Exodus 7-12).

These were signs to Pharaoh that he did not heed, and they cost him and the Egyptians dearly. Today we are getting signs of Jesus' coming, and we need to be ready for that event.

Many of these disasters and pestilences can be blamed on how we have managed our world. The Dust Bowl period of the 1930s was caused by the removing of topsoil and/or the overgrowing of crops, and not allowing land to sit unfarmed for about a year.

This farming act is called fallowing, which can be traced back to instructions God gave to the Israelites in Exodus 23:10-11, where they were told to plant and grow crops for six years, but then to leave the land fallow every seventh year. Part of the reason for the Dust Bowl years could be blamed on ignoring this basic fact of farming, causing the topsoil to become unable to grow crops.

The current China virus pandemic, its origin, and disputes of just how it became to even exist, is a major debate at the time of this writing. However, most agree that this virus was the result of the mishandling of research being performed at the Wuhan, China, Institute of Virology. Again, we can blame this pestilence on ourselves. Why such research was even being done, how the virus got loose from the lab, and how it infected humans so violently and quickly are unanswered today.

In the next chapter we will look at some of nature's pestilences that we deal with on a daily, yearly, and sometimes just occasional basis. Whether man-made or natural, these are some of the sorrows Jesus was talking about as signs of the end times.

Ever since sin came into the world, following Adam and Eve's sin in the garden of Eden, we have been inflicting ourselves with our own created pestilences. We are killing each other over control of an area of a city, the sale of drugs in a section or certain blocks, aborting babies just because a pregnancy was inconvenient, and the list goes on. But three issues are quite prominent today, and we have nobody to blame but ourselves and our sin nature.

Three Prominent Issues Today

One of these is known as the world's oldest profession, if we can call it that, prostitution, which includes pornography. The sex slave industry is becoming the most prominent in the sex world, and the victims are the young girls being forced into this world against their will. Supposedly, the Civil War was the end of slavery in the US, but many of the young women crossing our very porous southern border with Mexico are being brought across to be placed into this sex slavery business. Very few of these women will survive their slavery, and we cannot point anywhere but to ourselves for this crime against humanity.

Another misuse of our fellow humans involves the drug trade. Many of the members of the Mexican cartel are involved in the international transport of illegal drugs, and one of their cruel acts is to utilize humans as "mules" to move the drugs across the border. Then the drugs are readied for sale to people who are hooked on them. In the recent years, a Chinese-made drug called Fentanyl has entered this illegal business, and it kills thousands each year. All the cartels care about is getting their money for the drugs and ignore the fatal actions they are inflicting on the users.

The last of these humans-caused signs is quite controversial between the "straight" community, and the so-called "bent" community. I am referring to those who desire to live the LGBTQ+ lifestyle. The Bible is very clear about this sinful lifestyle, addressing that marriage is between a man and a woman only (Genesis 2:24; Matthew 19:3-7; Mark 10:6-10). Also, Paul identifies homosexuality as a sin (Romans 1:26-32; Ephesians 5:31). In other versions of the Bible, the Ephesians 5:31 verse reflects the word "sodomite," referring to the act of sodomy and the two cities of sin Sodom and Gomorrah in which homosexuality was rampant. It is one of the sins described in Genesis 19:4-5.

Many claim that Jesus never commented on the marriage issue; however, the Matthew and Mark references above are statements made by Jesus toward those Pharisees challenging His position against that of Moses. Further, Jesus made it clear that God the Father created us as male and females. This blows away the claims of many today, that there are more than two genders!

Despite these clear verses, many call Christians, and others too who oppose the LGBTQ+ lifestyle, as bigots and narrow-minded. Even some professing Christians feel that we are failing to show the love we are commanded in the second commandment to show to our neighbor (Exodus 20:6; Deuteronomy 5:10; Matthew 22:39). They feel we should be tolerant of those living a sinful lifestyle; however, nowhere in the Bible does it tell us to tolerate sin. We are only to love the sinner. In fact, God hates sin, as described in Proverbs 6:16-19!

Before we point fingers at each other, or blame the pestilences we are facing today on something else like climate change or some other nonexistent thing, we need to get things right between the person we see in the mirror and God. Do it today because there is no guarantee of a tomorrow.

10

Nature's Affect

Read Genesis 12; 26-50; the book of Ruth

Unlike the cause of the dust bowl period or the China virus addressed in the previous chapter, the volcanoes, tornadoes, and other weather-related occurrences are purely natural in their origin. Some affect us daily like rain or sunshine, some periodically like snowstorms. Each year from June 1 to the end of November is hurricane season, and then in some parts of the world cicadas arrive every seventeen years.

Some of these weather-related occurrences are no big deal, like a light rain, dusting of snow, etc. Thunderstorms can produce beneficial rain or flooding rains and even destructive tornadoes. Although not weather-related, the visit of the cicadas every seventeen years causes no disaster, but their never-ending sound for about a month can be quite annoying. Some natural occurrences, however, are calamitous. In 79 CE, Pompeii, Italy, was destroyed and buried under tons of ash from the volcano Mount Vesuvius' eruption.

An island near Indonesia completely disappeared when the volcano Krakatoa erupted in 1883 and killed over thirty-six thousand residents in that area. In this same area of the world, an earthquake occurred that caused a tsunami that killed about a quarter million people in 2004. Over long periods of time, tropical cyclones in the Atlantic Ocean and typhoons in the eastern Pacific Ocean deliver some of the most destructive winds and rain on Earth. Severe thunderstorms and tornadoes bring just as much damage but in a much shorter period.

The opposite problem, yet just as destructive, comes from the lack of rain resulting in famines. The Bible references for this chapter all surround situations as the result of famines. However, the loss of crops can also be the result of insects, like locust swarms, or even crickets like those experienced by the Mormons just after their arrival in Utah.

During the time Jesus was here on Earth, the Gospel writers record two occasions when Jesus calmed the Sea of Galilee from violent storms (Matthew 8:23-27; Mark 4:35-41). In fact, ever since the flood recorded in Genesis, Earth has been dealing with all sorts of natural catastrophic occurrences. Some we can forecast, especially with today's weather satellites. However, despite ground sensors, earthquakes and volcanic eruptions still catch us unprepared.

When Jesus was referring to pestilences in Matthew 24, He was talking about both natural and man-made. Just as God's warnings of the coming flood went unheeded by those who were on Earth, except for Noah and his family, the warning signs Jesus spoke about should be signs to all of us to be ready for the coming end times.

Satan is meddling with many minds today, blaming these more numerous occurrences of natural and man-made disasters on what scientists and others call global warming or climate change. These claims I call a total hoax, and as history shows, they are not becoming more frequent. They have existed since the flood that occurred about ten thousand years ago and continue with the hurricanes, volcano eruptions, and earthquakes documented year-round.

During the War of 1812, a hurricane helped save the United States from the invading British. As the British were closing in upon Washington, D.C. in 1814, a hurricane came onshore at that very time, just about wiped out the entire British military, and saved the capital and the nation. You might say that we were assisted with some divine intervention.

I have dealt with tornadoes and hurricanes during most of my years living in Texas. Hurricanes Carla and Beulah came onshore near Corpus Christi, Texas, and worked their way toward San Antonio, Texas, where my parents and I lived. Plus, these storms triggered several tornadoes in our area as well.

In a more recent occurrence, as Lori and I were driving home one day, we noticed a thunderstorm closing in on us. Suddenly, a tree fell across the road right in front of the car in front of us. Our car was bounced around, the lightning and thunder flashed and banged, and the rain came down hard. Later, we heard on our local weather station that a tornado had touched down not far away. The tracking of the storm was right across where we had been traveling. A funnel cloud had been over us, and we just missed being affected by a tornado.

In the two stories from Matthew and Mark I listed earlier, when some of Jesus' disciples shoved off onto the Sea of Galilee, the water was calm. However, the winds soon rose and made navigating the boat difficult and fearful. In the same way, when Lori and I were bouncing around in that car, I can assure you that we were not discussing what to have for supper!

The pestilences that Jesus spoke to the disciples about in Matthew 24, and to us today, were just some of the indications of the coming end times. Reader, they were then and are now meant to give us warnings of the imminent return of Jesus to rapture away His followers.

The question I would ask you is whether you know for a fact that you are ready for that time when Jesus returns? Matthew 24:36-37 make it very clear that God the Father only knows when that day will be. We need to be ready now because we may not have a then!

11

Opposing All Things Christian

Jesus continued instructing His disciples on signs of the end times and described the severe trials and tribulations His followers will experience. He explained that being a Christian will be very challenging in these end times. Many will be killed for the cause of Christ.

Little did His disciples realize that all them, except for John, would die in their service for preaching salvation through Jesus. We know that James, the brother of John, was beheaded by the Sanhedrin of the Jews (Acts 12:2), and Peter was crucified upside down on a cross (based on established church tradition). How the others died is at best legendary. John would live out his life in exile on the Greek island of Patmos.

All throughout history, many would die as servants of God. In addition to the disciples, Paul was beheaded following his imprisonment in Rome. Many Bible scholars believe Luke met this same fate. Before Paul's conversion on the Damascus Road, he was present at Stephen's stoning (Acts 7:54-60).

Since biblical times, millions have suffered for the cause of Christ, including being put to death. Some were hung, burned at the stake, beheaded, sawn in two, or drawn and quartered. Others died due to torture and imprisonment, including John's understudy named Polycarp. Later examples are William Tyndale and Eric Liddell.

Between the time Polycarp was burned at the stake and

when William Tyndale was hung for translating the Bible into English, very little is known about anything during the Middle Ages (500-1500 CE). Throughout the centuries, many have suffered for the cause of Christ, precisely what Jesus was telling His disciples while on the Mount of Olives (Matthew 24:1-14).

Extreme sacrifice was necessary in the United States' history to obtain freedom of religion and worship as directed in the Bible. The Pilgrims and Puritans left their homeland and sailed across the Atlantic Ocean to a new land they knew nothing about or would be prepared to deal with.

During WWII, many soldiers were tortured and imprisoned, and some died in captivity, like missionary Eric Liddell, who died in a Japanese prison camp near the war's end. We all know of the horrors of the Nazi's extermination of six million Jews, known as the Holocaust; however, the Germans placed numerous others including Christians in these facilities. Some like Corrie Ten Boom would survive by God's divine grace; others like her sister and the rest of her family did not.

Since those horrible years of WWII, the persecution of Christians, and all things associated with Christianity, has slowly increased. In 1963, the Supreme Court of the United States (SCOTUS) decided that prayer and Bible reading should be removed from public schools. In addition, since this ruling, this court and other federal courts have removed the teaching of God's creation from our schools and replaced it with teaching evolution (see my book *Creation Is a Science*). Multiple lawsuits have been filed to prevent prayer before games and Bible studies after the school day ended. These suits claim the mythical "separation of church and state" is constitutional. In my book *Confrontational Christianity*, I provide proof that this claim is not part of the constitution.

In recent years, numerous attempts have been made to eliminate all things Christmas from public view, including "Merry Christmas" greetings, nativity scenes displayed on public land, and even Christmas decorations on houses. Such holiday references supposedly offend others and their religious beliefs. These bans included Christian symbols such as Christian flags, Ten Commandment monuments or plaques, and crosses in cemeteries or open fields.

Church burnings also have become more frequent. Pastors are being warned about preaching against the LGBTQ+ lifestyle, as such preaching would be considered a hate crime. A teacher was ordered to remove her cross necklace because it was considered offensive. Even people holding signs opposing abortion are being harassed, yet the very act of aborting babies is being promoted by those in authority.

These examples are just a few of the "sorrows" Jesus was referring to when addressing His disciples. Some of our more modern sorrows may have not been known to the disciples, but our Lord Jesus Christ knew they were coming. We must resist Satan, his demons, and all those he utilizes to harass, verbally and physically attack, and even kill those serving the Lord. As a soldier of the cross, I get vicious posts directed at me and my stand for the cause of Christ. Some I just dismiss, but to others I make my stand very clear and do not back down. Remember, we are on the Lord's side, and as Paul wrote, "If God is for us, who can be against us?" (Romans 8:31)

12

A Fraction of Time

Read 1 Corinthians 15:50-54; Matthew 24:36-44, and 1 Thessalonians 4:13-5:11

Now we will get into the meat of this book. The Bible was written originally in Hebrew, Aramaic, and Greek. The New Testament was in Greek, then the whole Bible was translated into Latin, and then into German, English, and other languages.

First Corinthians 15:50-54 says the rapture will occur in what is described as "the twinkling of an eye." The original Greek word here is *Quotes Cosmos*, referring to a moment in time or "in the blink of an eye," hence the title of this book.

Until this point, we have looked at the physical makeup of the eye and the signs Jesus provided us of the coming end times. The timeframe between now and the beginning of the seven-year tribulation period (Matthew 24:15-35) is called the rapture.

In my book, *Time Witnessing*, I described how long it takes for an eye to blink: so fast that in the time you raise your hand, snap your fingers, and lower your hand again, about three raptures could have occurred. I learned this incredible fact from the informational papers the staff gave me during my initial visit to JH. When I put that information together with the

49

First Corinthians verses, even I was stunned by how short God's timeline is for us humans between now and the seven-year tribulation period.

Earlier I described several of what Jesus called "sorrows" that were signs of the coming end times. One concerned a deceiver who falsely claimed to be Jesus returned. In 1 Thessalonians 4:13-18, Paul addresses statements made to the people in this Greek city. False teachers had told the citizens that if their family members died, they would miss the rapture of those who believed and accepted Jesus as their Savior. Paul says this is not true; in fact, their family members who had already passed would be raised first, then the living believers would be caught up to meet them in the sky.

> *For the Lord Himself will descend from heaven with a shout, with the voice of an archangel, and with the trumpet of God. And the dead in Christ will rise first. Then we who are alive and remain shall be caught up together with them in the clouds to meet the Lord in the air. And thus we shall always be with the Lord. Therefore comfort one another with these words* (1 Thessalonians 4:16-18).

The actions in the verses above are significant because they describe the coming of Jesus into the clouds above the Mount of Olives, the shout of the archangel, and the sound of a trumpet that will begin the rapture. The dead who have believed in Jesus in the past will rise and come up first. Then we who are alive and believe will be caught up to meet Jesus and the others. Finally, all of us will go with Jesus into heaven. All of this will occur in a fraction of a second, so fast that it will probably take the news about fifteen minutes to even realize this happened worldwide.

Next, in 1 Thessalonians 5:1-11, Paul expands his description of the rapture and why we must always be ready. He describes this event as the same way a thief comes to perform a crime.

His point here is two-fold. First, to prevent the thief from being successful, we should always be vigilant to maintain the security around our household and belongings. Secondly, he wants us to understand that we must always be ready because a thief will come when we least expect it.

The first step in being ready is knowing that we have accepted Jesus as our personal Savior. I accepted Jesus as my Savior at a church camp in Texas in 1966. Reader, how about you? Have you prayed to accept Jesus, asked Him to forgive your sins, and asked Him to become the Lord of your life? If so, you have received salvation, which is required for us to be personally ready for the rapture.

In Acts 1:8, Jesus commands His followers to be witnesses for Him, which is called the Great Commission. Preparing for this time includes doing all we can to know our family members, coworkers, friends, and others we meet are also ready. Now I am not saying we all must be Billy Graham. Instead, when the opportunity presents itself, tell others about Jesus and why you want them to be saved.

Understand, do not disrupt your workday but ask if you can meet to talk at an acceptable time and place. Not all us will be great witnesses, but just sharing what Jesus has done for us is our calling. For example, as I stated in my dedication to this book, the writing of my books is my best manner of witnessing. Check out my website, www.timewitnessing.com.

All Jesus asks us to do is witness for Him, and if the person you talk to chooses to say no, or outright rejects Jesus, that is on them, not you, and they will have to answer for that decision. In the next chapter, I will explain this part of witnessing in more detail. Make sure you are ready today because the next hour may not be in your future.

13

Home of the Redeemed

Read Romans 14:10-13; 2 Corinthians 5; and Revelation 19:7-9

The *Merriam-Webster* online dictionary defines redeemed as "being freed from the consequences of sin." It means justified, sanctified, and released from our sins. After the rapture, we who are taken into heaven with Jesus will spend the next seven years participating in two events. Here on Earth, though, the horrors of the tribulation period will be taking place.

In chapter 12, I described that Jesus commanded His disciples, and us today, to be witnesses for Him. When we enter the heavenly realm of our Savior, we will be partakers in two significant events. The first of these events is described in the Romans and 2 Corinthians references above.

This first event was recorded in the original Greek by the word *bema*. A bema seat was a place of judgment and is best translated as "the judgment seat of Christ." When we accept Jesus as our Savior, part of that act is asking for forgiveness of our sins. In Psalm 103:12, we are assured of forgiveness, as it says our sins are removed "as far as the east is from the west." Geographically, east never meets west! So, our sins will not be judged when we come before this judgment seat. As far as God and our Savior are concerned, they no longer exist. This does not mean we can live like the devil once we are saved! Instead, when we sin later, and we will, we need only confess that sin as described in 1 John 1:9.

Each of us will come before this judgment seat to have our service for Jesus reviewed. Those acts we did as witnesses for Jesus will be seen in the same manner as gold, silver, and precious stones like diamonds and rubies. Those areas where we failed in our service will be looked upon as hay, wood, and stubble (1 Corinthians 3:5-15).

Our failures will be burned as a loss, but we will only be rewarded for those services for Jesus. However, we will give these rewards back to Jesus because His sacrifice on the cross made it possible for us to be saved and spend eternity in heaven.

As children of God, we will often refer to each other as brothers or sisters in Christ. However, we are called the church or bride of Christ in the Bible, as in the Revelation verses above. Following the judgment seat of Christ, we come to the more celebrative event in heaven.

The Church

When the writers of the Bible, directed by God, refer to the church, they mean believers and not the buildings in which believers met to worship. Jesus came to Earth and sacrificed His life on that cross for us, His church, and He rose again on the third day to deliver us from our sins. He died to rescue His bride from the clutches of sin.

Once we have come together in heaven, we will celebrate this event like the reception that follows a wedding between the bridegroom, Jesus, and His church, His bride. This wonderful event is called the marriage supper of the Lamb. Jesus was the Lamb sent by His Father to be the sacrifice for all the world's sins (John 3:16). Following the judgment seat of Christ, the redeemed in heaven will come together to this grand supper where we celebrate our residence in heaven for all eternity.

The Bible does not detail this supper except to record that it will occur, and Jesus our Savior and Lord will be the host. I can only imagine that this supper will be more extravagant than any formal meal we have ever attended. Further, the menu will feature the very best of everything in God's creation.

The setting for this supper will be within all the glories of heaven. One can allow one's imagination to go wild here, as we will be seated at this wondrous event with the Who's Who from the Bible—notables like Noah, Abraham, King David and prophets like Isaiah, Jeremiah, and Malachi. Then from the New Testament times come the disciples including Paul, Timothy, Luke, and my personal mentor, Peter.

However, what makes this event is that we are with our Savior and Lord Jesus Christ. Without His willing sacrifice on the cross and His resurrection on what we call Easter Sunday, none of us would have ever seen the glories of heaven. Yes, it will be a wonderous celebration, and as I write these words, all I can say is, "Even so, come, Lord Jesus!" (Revelation 22:20)

14

Horrors on Horseback

Read Matthew 24:15-28 and Revelation 6:1-8.

As joyous and wonderful as the time the believers will have in heaven, the next seven years on Earth will be just the opposite. The persecutions, threats of terrorism, food shortages, and violent crime and killings will not match the tribulation period experiences.

The Bible describes this period in two phases. The first three-and-a-half years are called the tribulation, and the second three-and-a-half years are called the *great* tribulation. Also, God will deal with these seven years with three sets of woes, which are the seven seal judgments, the seven trumpet judgments, and the seven bowl judgments. These judgments are progressive, each one worse than the one before.

The first four seal judgments are known as the four horsemen of the apocalypse. At the opening of the first seal, we are introduced to a rider on a white horse. This is the coming one world leader referred to as the conqueror, better known as the Beast or the Antichrist (1 John 2:18; 2 John 1:7). This first horseman is an actual living person and will probably be well-known to the world; however, the Bible does not give us a name other than the Beast or the Antichrist.

This first horseman will become the one world leader over

all nations, he will conquer all who oppose him. He will have authority over all weapons and military personnel. Unlike the other riders we will cover in this chapter, he will rule over the whole Earth for the entire seven years of the tribulation period. The Antichrist will be indwelt by Satan, and he will oversee the bloodiest time ever known on Earth. His deeds, and those under his direction, will terrorize the population that are left in ways never seen or witnessed until that time.

The next horseman is riding a red horse and has a sword in his hand. Upon this second seal, a worldwide war will begin, killing millions. Part of this worldwide war will bring all opposing nations and people under the rule of Antichrist; the other part will result in the destruction of life that the Antichrist brings to this period on Earth.

The third seal brings a rider on a black horse, and he has a set of scales with him. Following the worldwide war brought on by the red horse rider, the availability of food, crops, etc., will become very scarce, and famine will be experienced over the whole Earth. In the Revelations 6 Scripture reading, the cost of minimal quantities of basic bread-making grain was a "denarius," which at that time was equal to a day's wages. As a result of this third seal, a person will earn only enough to feed themself and nobody else in their family.

The fourth seal brings a rider on a pale horse, and he has the name "death." This rider combines all the previous riders' actions. One-fourth of the population will be killed from the wars, famine, and destruction Antichrist brings upon the world.

These riders will be responsible for only the beginning of the woes people living in the tribulation period will experience. What makes this period so much worse than the times we live in today is that the age of God's grace upon the Earth ended with the rapture of the believers. Now, all that remains on Earth are the true colors of Satan. The full wrath of God against sin is being released upon those who chose not to believe or outright rejected His offer of salvation.

The Beast will be the servant of Satan himself and will rule the entire world as Satan directs him to do. The other three riders are members of Satan's demonic host. In Revelation 12:7-9, we are told of a war in heaven, led by the archangel Lucifer, also known as Satan. This conflict is believed to have occurred before time began, as described in Genesis 1. This is since Satan, who dwelled in the serpent who tempted Eve in the garden of Eden, had already been cast out of heaven by then.

Along with Lucifer, one-third of the angelic host followed him and were also cast out of heaven. These followers became Satan's demonic host, of which these three riders are a part. These four horsemen make up the first seal judgments; however, the woes experienced during this tribulation period have only begun.

The fifth seal (Revelation 6:9-11) turns our view into the heavenly realm and to those martyred in the cause of Christ. They ask when their deaths will be avenged, and the response to them reflects the woes to come to those still alive on Earth. These martyrs include those killed honoring God and His Son Jesus in their works and deeds, from Abel to our modern day. However, we learn in verse eleven that even more will face death for service to God during this period of horror.

Over the thousands of years, both men and women have lost their lives as martyrs for God, some just because they were Christians. In recent years, minority Christians living around

Mosul, Iraq (perhaps descendants of the ancient city of Nineveh from the book of Jonah), were slaughtered for their faith by members of the Islamic State of Iraq and Syria (ISIS). Several members of the Coptic Christian community in Egypt were beheaded by the Muslim Brotherhood for the same reason. Based on these verses, many more people who come to faith during the tribulation period will also face martyrdom. They will come to believe in Jesus through the witnesses we address in the next chapter.

The sixth seal (Revelation 6:12-17) features the first worldwide calamity, a global earthquake that moves mountains and other land masses out of place. The sun is turned black and the moon red. The massive amount of hysteria will drive everybody from kings to servants and enslaved people to wherever they can go, pleading for rocks, etc., to cover them and protect them from the wrath of God. Despite these worldwide destructive actions under this seal, people who were left behind, having not accepted Jesus or rejected Him, will have only begun to experience the wrath of God.

15

The Witnesses

Read Revelation 7:1-8; 8:1-6; and 14:1-5

After the first six seals, we are introduced to an extensive group of missionaries totaling one hundred forty-four thousand. These missionaries are from the twelve Jewish tribes listed in the Revelation 7 reading above, and from each tribe twelve thousand.

These missionaries are commissioned to only a specific people left behind following the rapture. During this period on Earth, some people will never have heard the message of salvation in Jesus Christ. Missionaries will bring the saving news to these folks, and they will be sealed by God. Then the Antichrist cannot harm them.

Wearing a seal on their forehead (Revelation 14), these witnesses will spread out over the Earth with the saving news to those who never heard. With all the radio, television, and internet access available today, it might be hard for some of us to understand how some people have never heard about the Bible or the Gospel of Jesus Christ. But in many countries today, possession of even part of the Bible could result in imprisonment or even death. Also, television and internet access are blocked or even nonexistent outside of what that nation's leadership wants its population to know or hear.

As these witnesses proceed throughout the Earth, the seventh and final seal will be opened in heaven. At first, there is total silence for one-half hour. Then seven angels are presented with seven trumpets representing the next series of woes upon the Earth. However, before they begin, another angel will cause lightning, thunder, and another earthquake to strike the Earth. The witnesses will continue their ministry to those who need to hear about Jesus, undeterred by the seventh seal on the planet.

Looking at events in the Bible and even in today's world, many times we wonder about how and why God directed or allowed some events to occur. The same will be true during this period when the witnesses bring the news to those they are commissioned.

Just because God has sealed these witnesses does not mean those who believe and accept Jesus as their Savior will be spared the acts of Antichrist. Remember with the fifth seal, the martyrs were told that others were yet to come, and they will be put to death by Antichrist.

The Age of Grace

I do not want you the reader to be confused by what you have read to this point. We now live in what is called the age of grace on Earth, also referred to as the dispensation of grace or the church age. It is generally considered to have begun around Pentecost when Peter gave his call for everyone to accept Jesus in Acts 2:14-39.

Right now, the desire of God and His Son is that all us accept Jesus as Savior and Lord of our lives. However, after the rapture occurs, only those who have not heard of the saving knowledge of Jesus will have the opportunity to accept Him during the tribulation period.

I have asked you to accept Jesus as your Savior several times already in this book. If you decide to hold off or reject Jesus, after the rapture you will not have the chance to accept Him. You see, through this book you have heard the way of salvation through Jesus and cannot claim otherwise later. I urge you to accept Jesus as your Savior now because you may not have the next hour or even the next minute to think about it!

16

The Trumpet Woes

Read Revelation 8:7-13 and Revelation 9

The next series of woes are known as the trumpet judgments, and the old cliché, "You ain't seen nothing yet," applies. In these judgments, as angels sound their respective trumpets, a new and progressively worse woe comes upon the Earth. These judgments do not affect God's witnesses nor any of those who accepted Jesus as Savior and received His seal. The converts are not subject to God's judgments; however, they can be killed by the Antichrist and become martyrs for their acceptance of Jesus Christ.

The first trumpet sounding causes hail, fire, and blood to fall to Earth, burning up all the grass and one-third of the trees. The charring of the grass and trees will bring real climate change. The Earth will experience a deadly increase in carbon dioxide. Breathing clean air will become increasingly difficult and affect both animals and humans.

The second trumpet sounding accompanies a fiery mountain falling to Earth. This will cause one-third of the fish and sea life to die, making one-third of the oceans and seas to become blood. One-third of sailing ships will be destroyed, which causes additional loss of food and survival goods that happened to be cargo on those ships.

A flaming star, possibly a meteor named Wormwood, arrives at the sounding of the third trumpet. This flaming star will cause all sources of fresh water still in existence to become bitter, and for those who are not sealed, drinking water will be eliminated.

The fourth trumpet sounding will take away one-third of the sun, moon, and stars. With this woe, diminished sunshine will have adverse effects on the Earth. Also, an angel will fly over the land as an eagle soaring, warning of the coming trumpet woes still to come. No efforts by the Antichrist or his followers can prevent the woes or their effects from coming.

Another star arrives with the fifth Trumpet sounding, and it possesses the keys to the bottomless pit. Upon opening this pit, a thick furnace-like smoke will be so thick that it darkens the sun and moon. Locusts with tails like scorpions will emerge from the smoke, and they will not eat the grass, plants, or trees. Instead, their mission will be to torment those who do not bear the seal.

These scorpions are not to kill but to bring the torment of their stingers into those without the seal for five months. These folks will seek a way to die; however, they will not find the ability to do so and will suffer the locust's torment without relief. In Revelation 9:7-10, the hideous description of what these locusts looked and sounded like is something out of the scariest horror movie ever seen. The locust from the pit has a king. In Hebrew, his name is Abaddon, translated as "destruction or doom." In Greek, his name is Apollyon, translated as "destroyer." Both names refer to the archangel from the pit, Satan himself.

Revelation 9:12 warns that one woe has passed and two more are to come. With this warning, the sixth trumpet is sounded in heaven, and the angel who blows this trumpet is instructed to release the four "angels" (demons) from the river Euphrates.

Again, John writes down from his vision that these four "angels" lead an army of over two hundred million and describes in detail the appearance of the horses (Revelation 9:15-19). With this release, this incredible army will kill one-third of those remaining on Earth without the seal. Despite all these woes to date, those who still survived without the seal remained unchanged in their worship of idols made from many precious metals and stones, and these unrepentant continue their sinful deeds and actions under the Antichrist.

Following the two witnesses we will read about in the next chapter, the seventh trumpet will sound. In Revelation 11:14, the second woe will have passed, and a third is coming soon. Then the seventh trumpet sounds, and the glory of heaven is revealed. Meanwhile, the tribulation period on Earth is coming to an end, and the great tribulation period is about to begin.

17

The Two Witnesses

Read Revelation 11:1-13

In chapter 15, we read about the one hundred forty-four thousand witnesses who will bring the word about Jesus to those who have never heard. Now in this chapter we will meet two special witnesses sent by God to warn people of the woes that are coming. The reading for this chapter tells us what the witnesses preach, what they can do, how the Antichrist will deal with them, and how God's Word gets through to the people left behind.

The Bible does not tell us the names of these witnesses, just as we are not given the name of the Antichrist, the Beast on the white horse. However, many have their opinions who they might be, based on what they are sent to do. Dr. David Jeremiah believes they will be Moses and Elijah, the same two Bible characters who appeared with Jesus at His transfiguration (Matthew 17:1-13; Luke 9:28-36).

I also have an opinion of who these witnesses may be, but their identity is not important, but their witness to the people is. The Bible describes two people who never died but whom God brought up to heaven. The first was Enoch (Genesis 5:18-24). The other was Elijah, whom God brought up to heaven in a whirlwind accompanied by a fiery chariot and horses (2 Kings 2:1-11).

In our reading for this chapter, God describes these witnesses as two olive trees and lampstands standing before the Earth—obvious metaphors for two strong representatives of God against the Antichrist and human beings. If anyone tries to silence the witnesses, God gave them the ability to defend themselves by fire from their mouths. In this way, they can really toast their attackers.

These witnesses will preach for 1,260 days, or three-and-a-half years, the period known as the tribulation. In addition to their God-given defenses, God gave them power over the weather. They can turn the water into blood and can cause plagues as often as they desire. To the people, these witnesses are formidable foes.

Nobody, including the Antichrist, can oppose these witnesses when they are commissioned by God. At the end of their testimony to the Earth, warning of events to come, the Antichrist will be able to kill the witnesses. Their dead bodies will remain in place for three-and-a half days unburied, so all the world can see them.

I saw the Temple Mount in Jerusalem and the Wailing Wall during my two tours to Israel. This area is where I believe the witnesses will bring their testimony to the Earth, where they will be killed and left to lay for three-and-a-half days.

This location is so prominent even today because the Temple Mount is holy to three worldwide religions. It is Islam's third most religious site. It is the sight of Solomon's temple and the Holy of Holies, sacred to the Jews. Finally, it and Jerusalem are sacred to Christianity.

Because of the location's prominence, the witnesses' dead bodies can and probably will be televised worldwide by the Antichrist. In this way, the Antichrist can gloat over conquering God's witnesses.

John records that during the three-and-a-half days the dead witnesses lay in public view, people will celebrate their deaths and will exchange gifts as is done for birthdays or Christmas. However, at the end of the three-and-a-half days, the celebrating will abruptly stop when the witnesses stand up. Then all the people will hear a voice from heaven calling them up, and they will rise in a cloud and disappear.

Upon the departure of the witnesses, a great earthquake will occur, destroying one-tenth of Jerusalem and killing seven thousand. Those remaining will praise God at that time. This event marks the end of two woes, and the third woe is coming. At this time the seventh trumpet we read about in the previous chapter will sound.

18

The Beast and False Prophet

Read Revelation chapter 13 and 14:6-11

In chapter 4, you read about the vision of Daniel and a creature coming out of the water with ten large horns and a smaller horn. We have now reached the point of the second three-and-a-half years, also called the great tribulation. Here Daniel's vision will become a reality for those still alive on Earth after the seal and trumpet judgments.

Revelation 13 describes Daniel's vision, by John, of a creature rising out of the water with ten large horns. A smaller horn was wounded and shouted blasphemous words toward God. On the ten large horns are crowns, representing the ten kings subject to the smaller horn, representing the Antichrist. The rider on the white horse is gravely wounded but is healed by what John calls the dragon, or Satan.

In the best-selling book series *Left Behind*, the Antichrist is correctly described as having been killed; upon the literal indwelling of the now dead, Satan resurrects the Beast. This is done to show those still alive on Earth that he can also rise from the dead. Therefore, the Bible reading states that he was healed by the dragon.

The horrors of this time on Earth will be headed up by Satan, the Antichrist or Beast, and a spokesman for the Beast called the False Prophet. Jesus warned of this unholy alliance that would bring destruction to the world during the tribulation period. The False Prophet can perform actions such as causing fire and act as the Beast's mouthpiece.

We are not given the name of the False Prophet. This will be a real person who will act like one who preaches and teaches the will of the Beast. Plus, he will direct the construction of a large image of the Beast for all to worship. This False Prophet will be granted power to give a voice to the image so it can speak to the people on Earth. To those who refuse to worship the image of the Beast, the False Prophet will kill them.

In Revelation 13:16-18 and chapter 14, we are told that the False Prophet will initiate the requirement for all to obtain the mark of the Beast. This mark will be applied to the forehead or back of the right hand, and nobody can buy or sell without this mark. The Bible clarifies that those who receive this mark will suffer eternal condemnation in the pit known as hell. Those who are saved during this period must also refrain from this mark, or they will also be condemned.

Through the last one hundred or more years, many have evaluated those who they feel might fit the characteristics of the Antichrist or the False Prophet. In the mid-1900s, most were convinced that Adolf Hitler, Benito Mussolini, or Emperor Hirohito would fit into this description. Some even labeled President Franklin Delano Roosevelt or Josef Stalin in this group. Especially after the establishment of the State of Israel in May 1948, the guessing only increased. Decades later, Nikita Khrushchev and Mao Zedong could have been considered qualified for this role. Even today many world leaders are suspected as the possible culprit.

In *Left Behind*, a fictional book series based on Revelation, the authors gave the False Prophet role to the sitting Pope. However, he was replaced by another fictional character. The authors I have read on end times prophecy all seem to direct their aim to a religious leader during the tribulation period. No one leader can be labeled with this evil position. However, a Bible-teaching, born-again minister of God's Word certainly will not be on Earth to even fill this place during the tribulation. I hesitate to name names here; however, leaders of false religions would qualify for this position next to the Beast.

A current world leader, an internationally known person like an ambassador or head of a world body may very well be the future Antichrist or Beast. It is also possible that the leader of one of the world's false, idol worshiping religions could be the future False Prophet. The Bible only gives their characteristics, not their names.

Another sign we can look at as part of the coming end times is the existence of microchip technology. For many years, dogs and cats have been chipped with a microchip containing the owner's name, address, and contact information. If they get lost or run away, a veterinarian's office or organizations like the Society for the Prevention of Cruelty to Animals (SPCA) can scan the animal and obtain the owner's information. This information can be updated in case of a change in ownership.

In more recent years, the country of Sweden has been experimenting with implanting chips into humans. In Revelation 14:6-11, we read that part of the mark will be the Beast's number, 666. The fact that such technology exists today should give us reason to contemplate the end times. The rapture is imminent and not years away.

71

The Number 666

Before I bring this chapter to a close, I want to share an idea I have about why the Beast's number will be 666. I shared the history of our adversary Satan, noting that he was originally one of God's created heavenly host, and in fact one of the three archangels. He, Lucifer, led a revolt wanting to replace God. He and one-third of the angels were cast out of heaven. First defeat!

In Matthew 4:1-11, we learn of Satan's temptation of Jesus. Then in several books of the New Testament, we read of Jesus' crucifixion on a Roman cross. However, Jesus rose from the dead on the third day, defeating sin and death. This guaranteed eternity in heaven for all who accept Jesus as their Savior. Second defeat for Satan!

A future chapter will address the millennial kingdom of Jesus, and how at the end of that one-thousand-year kingdom Satan will be released from the pit, gather an army of unbelievers from that time, and revolt against Jesus—only to be defeated and cast into hell for eternity. Third and final defeat of Satan!

God's number, sometimes referred to by Christians as the perfect number because God is perfect, is seven. He created all things in six days and rested on the seventh day. The Sabbath Day was holy in Old Testament times. Satan failed to defeat God and His Son Jesus three times, coming short of his own perfection, so his number is 666. Reader, Satan's fate in hell is stuck, but yours need not be. Accept Jesus as your Savior today, and eternity in heaven is guaranteed for you.

19

The Bowl Judgments

Read Revelation chapters 15-18

When a new movie is about to be released, or a new television show is about to premiere, we often see trailers of the coming release. These are created to draw and entice people to go watch this new release. Then before the movie starts or the television show begins, several commercials or promotions are always presented. Their purpose is to cause us to be on the edge of our seats in anticipation.

In the case of these final woes, the chapter 15 reading is almost like one of these trailers. Actions are ongoing in heaven, making ready the seven bowl judgments. However, people still alive are again in the position of not knowing the terrible things ahead. The seven final judgments on the Earth, and those who rejected Jesus, will bring the great tribulation to the point where the end of God's wrath will culminate in a final battle between good and evil.

These bowl judgments will affect everyone except God's witnesses and those who have received Jesus during the tribulation period, including the Beast and his False Prophet. With these judgments, the full wrath of God will set in and be realized by everyone still alive. Revelation 16 describes these judgments to us and why you do not want to be on Earth during this time.

The angel with the first bowl pours out its contents. This causes a "foul and loathsome" sore to form on all with the mark of the Beast and those who worship him. Here God applies His wrath to the survivors for accepting the Beast's mark and worshiping him instead of God Almighty. The angel with the second bowl poured its contents upon the waters of Earth, killing every living thing in them and causing the water to turn bloody. The third angel poured its bowl, and all the rivers and springs on Earth were also turned to blood.

The angel with the fourth bowl poured out its contents, which caused the sun to become scorching; those with the mark were scorched by the sun. They cursed God, who caused these plagues to come upon them. Then the angel with the fifth bowl poured out its contents, causing darkness all over the Earth. They had sores, were in pain, and made no effort to repent of anything they said or did.

With that angel's sixth bowl poured out, the river Euphrates will dry up. Then the unholy alliance will release messengers like frogs to call the armies of the Beast to the battle in the place called Armageddon.

The Seventh Bowl

The angel with the seventh and final bowl then pours its contents upon the Earth. This judgment brings the worst earthquake to Earth and destroys the Beast's capital, the new Babylon. Along with these destructions, a great hailstorm comes down, with hailstone weighing more than one hundred pounds.

John then shares another vision. One of the angels who delivered the bowl judgments showed John a woman (identified as a harlot) riding on a ten-horned beast from the pit. In the chapter 17 reading, this vision, and the surrounding waters, are metaphorical for the Beast, Babylon, and what these characters did to those who accepted Jesus during the tribulation period. In the vision, the woman holds a cup with the martyr's blood that the Beast killed.

Finally, Revelation 18 concerns Babylon's destruction and all it stands for as the Beast's capital. It reflects the laments of all who survived the tribulation and their sorrow at the city's loss. The Beast led the lost to take his mark and worship him. They now see that all is gone that they held as holy. They realize their fate is set too late, and all hope is gone.

Reader, all these judgments are still future. Right now, you can avoid these seven years of horror, pain, and calamity. Those who survive will know that all is hopeless, and what they will have probably denied up until now is about to become real. You can spend this time in heaven at that grand supper with a simple prayer. I plead with you to do it now because I do not want you to endure these seven years of tribulation.

20
The Ultimate Showdown
Read Revelation 19:11 - 20:10

In modern-day Israel, located between Mount Megiddo and the city of Nazareth, is a vast valley that is a prime agricultural region of Israel. This is what is known as the Valley of Jezreel and is mentioned in the Bible in Joshua 17:16, Judges 6:33, and Hosea 1:5. This valley is referred to in Hebrew as *Har Megiddo*, from which the name Armageddon originates. This Hebrew word means "Mount Megiddo." The word Armageddon is mentioned only once in the Bible, in Revelation 16:16, part of the reading in the previous chapter.

In the Old West, as seen in many western movies and television shows, the good guy and bad guy would settle their disagreement with a shootout. These showdowns were sometimes a special event that brought out the townspeople. This type of event also occurred during the Civil War, when the local town folks would have picnics while the soldiers from the North and South fought it out on the battleground.

The event described in this chapter has no viewers. Instead, all will be involved in some manner, including our Lord and Savior and the redeemed. The end has come for the Beast, False Prophet, and all those who have the mark.

The sixth bowl in the previous chapter has demonic creatures like frogs calling the armies of the Earth to Armageddon where the Beast and False Prophet's military force opposes Jesus and the heavenly host. It is not hard to imagine the massive number of soldiers and military hardware that will assemble in this valley when you consider the weapons that many nations today manufacture every year and sell to other countries around the world.

Despite all the millions who died during the seven-year tribulation period, the Bible tells us the Beast will still have a great army at his disposal to war against the forces of heaven. However, this battle will be a concise one. John's description from his vision is that of a sword from the mouth of Jesus. This is a symbolic reference to the Word of God, described as a two-edged sword in Hebrews 4:12.

According to *Britannica* online, the Anglo-Zanzibar War was the shortest in history to date, having lasted only one hour. When Jesus speaks the Word of God when He arrives at this valley, this record will be smashed in a big way and will kill the entire army of the Beast. Revelation 14:20 says the result of this battle will cause the blood, called the results of the "wine press," to be as deep as a horse's bridle, which is about five feet. Those of the heavenly host (which I pray will be you along with me) will each have our own white horse like that of Jesus; we will just watch as this battle is settled by our Lord in a moment.

Then an angel, as described in Revelation 19:17-19, will call the "birds" of the world to come to the feast, which will be the aftermath of Armageddon. Many years ago, a report was released about this valley's inordinately large number of vultures. During one of my tours of Israel, some vultures were pointed out to our group. Seeing just how large this valley is and imagining it being five feet deep in blood with dead soldiers all around, makes me shudder about the end of the tribulation period.

After the battle, the Beast and the False Prophet will be cast into hell. For eternity they will suffer for their actions along with anyone who rejected Jesus as Savior.

The result of this battle will see the deaths of all who did not accept Jesus, not just the military soldiers. Those who somehow survived the horrors of the judgments and the seven-year tribulation period will now face death before facing a much different judgment seat. Also, Satan will be locked away in the pit for one thousand years and has no authority to tempt those who received Jesus during this period. One thousand years of peace will have come to Earth.

21

Jesus, King of Kings and Lord of Lords

Read Revelation 20

All the events described in this book are yet to occur. Writing under the direction and authority of God, John was told to record his vision of the future for our benefit. Since he did, we can understand why we want to avoid these scenarios. This is why I have urged you to accept Jesus as your Savior, so you will evade the tribulation period and all its judgments.

After the seven years of these horrible judgments, the next period in God's timeline is a one-thousand-year time of total peace on Earth, called the millennium. We have done quite a bit of imagining how the world will be, and this period of peace will be no exception.

In preparing this chapter, I thought about the most peaceful place I have ever visited in my many travels. I thought of the Wailea Canyon on the island of Kauai in Hawaii, the silence of the battlefield in Gettysburg, Pennsylvania, and the wonderful feeling I had standing on the summit of the Mount of Olives in Israel. I recall the soft sounds of the canyon waterfalls, the eerie quiet of that battlefield, and the unspoken joy of standing on top of the Mount of Olives.

None of these places will measure up to the peace and

wonders of the thousand-year reign of Jesus Christ on Earth. Gone is the evil of the Beast and the False Prophet, and any influence by Satan and his demons is nonexistent. Peace presides because Jesus will oversee the whole Earth. This contrasts with what the Beast brought upon the Earth and God's wrath on people who chose to not accept His Son. All the wrongs, diseases, and problems that sin brought into the world will disappear. No more animal threats will be possible during this time (see Isaiah 11:6; 65:25).

One aspect of life that will not be gone is couples having babies. The remnant of believers who survive to the end of the tribulation years will be the only ones who can continue to procreate. Those of us who are of the heavenly host will have glorified bodies that are the same as Jesus' upon His resurrection.

All those who passed before the rapture, all the characters from the Bible, and our family and friends will be part of this incredible time of peace, led by our Savior and Lord.

You might be wondering what we will be doing during these years. Well, the Bible does not give us such details; however, I am sure we will not be just laying around on hammocks and sipping iced tea.

Another question about the kingdom might be how Jesus will set up His government in the Millennium. In Revelation 20:4, the word "thrones" is used, and it says the martyrs "reigned with Him." No more specifics are given. We do know that Jesus will reign as King over the whole Earth. If He appoints others to oversee areas of the kingdom, only then will we know.

Verses 1-3 and 7-10 detail the locking away of Satan. However, after one thousand years, he will be rereleased for "a little while." All of us have those times when we question why something happens. Why Satan is released at this point is one of mine. I have already given you my opinion of why Satan's number is 666. Well, here is where he earns that last 6.

The sons and daughters of believers who survived the tribulation were born with the sinful nature we inherited from Adam and Eve in the garden of Eden. Therefore, these sons and daughters will be tempted by Satan, and he will be able to assemble an enormous army Scripture compares to "the sands of the sea." But, like the brief time it took for the result of the battle of Armageddon, fire will be sent down from heaven and will destroy Satan's final attempt against God.

Satan becomes powerless and will join the Beast and the False Prophet in hell, where they will be eternally tormented. However, they are about to be joined by countless people who did not accept Jesus as their Savior throughout thousands of years of humanity.

In the same way as believers of this time, the age of grace will come before Jesus at the judgment seat of Christ in heaven. Anyone who has not believed in Him will come before Jesus at their own judgment seat. This judgment is the great white throne judgment. Everyone will come before Jesus in-dividually. Anyone who does not have their name recorded in the Book of Life, also called Lamb's Book of Life, will be cast into the lake of fire, also called hell. Along with Satan, his de-mons, the Beast, and the False Prophet, they will suffer the torment of hell for eternity.

How long is eternity? Forever seems like such a simple an-swer, but it is very accurate. A more descriptive answer, though, would be a period with a beginning but no end. See my book *Time Witnessing* for more information on this description.

Often the words "The End" appear at the close of older movies. That is where we are now, at the end of time as we know it. In the final two chapters of Revelation, we will learn about the glory and beauty of the new heaven and Earth. This reward is why you need to accept Jesus as Savior, avoid the tribulation, be part of all God has for believers, and spend eternity with Him. Do it now. Tomorrow may be too late.

22

New Heaven, New Earth

Read Revelation 21 and 22

On Earth today, many buildings are wonders of construction and beauty, with contents just as beautiful. I am told that both Buckingham Palace in London, England, and the Palace at Versailles in France, are stunning buildings of construction outside and inside. However, the structure considered the most beautiful, as well as the most expensive to build, is that of the Taj Mahal in India. In fact, the Taj Mahal is one of the seven wonders of the modern world. Others are the statue of Christ the Redeemer on the mountain overlooking Rio de Janeiro in Brazil, and the red rock city of Petra in Jordon. Some have added an eighth wonder, that of the Astrodome in Houston, Texas.

None of these buildings, in fact any of the wonders over the centuries including the wonders of the ancient world will match the indescribable beauty of our future heavenly home, described in chapter 21. The Bible tells us, based on what the angel told John to record, that the new heaven we will be taken to at the rapture, will be replaced by a new heaven and a new Earth. What the new Earth will be like is not specified, except that there will not be any "sea." However, upon it will sit the new heaven.

Its magnificence is surpassed only by its size. In verse 16 of chapter 21, we are told that the walls are 12,000 furlongs high, wide, and long, which in miles is 1,500 miles high, wide, and long. That is an exact square about the distance from Maine to Florida, over to Texas, up to Minnesota, and back over to Maine; and just as high as well. In the next verse, 21:17, we read that the walls are 144 cubic thick, which using eighteen inches as a cubic, equals 216 feet thick.

The walls are made of Jasper, and heaven itself of pure gold, described as "clear as glass." Verses 19 and 20 tell us that the new heaven will sit on twelve precious stone foundations, one each for the twelve disciples. Then in verse 21, we are told that the twelve gates of the new heaven were each made of a single pearl, representing the twelve tribes of the Jews.

In John 14:2, Jesus said that in His Father's house (heaven) exist many mansions and that He will prepare these dwelling places for us. God will be the light that illuminates heaven, and no sin will exist there. No sorrow, tears, or sadness will be part of our eternal life in heaven. This is the forever reward for those who accept Jesus as Savior and Lord.

John 22 tells us of a pure river in the middle of heaven, which is the River of Life from God. Trees line the river, bearing fruit along with their leaves. This almost indescribable place is why we Christians long for the rapture and the reward of living in our heavenly home.

The final verses of that chapter say three times that Jesus is coming soon. Reflecting on Matthew chapter 24:36, nobody except God the Father knows when the rapture, or the beginning of the tribulation sorrows, will begin. That is why we must be ready to avoid the horrors of those seven years plus eternity in hell.

Some readers may think I have written this book to scare people. I could have just made you aware of the coming end times and left out the details. The reason I describe specifics is to give you further understanding of why you want to be ready for Jesus' coming.

Why tell you that a train is coming down the tracks or watch out for coming cars down a street, without you understanding the deadly consequences for ignoring the oncoming dangers? The same is true about the coming rapture of the followers of Jesus. By not knowing the consequences of not accepting Him or rejecting Him outright, you are condemning yourself to an eternity in hell.

Unlike those who have already sealed their fate in hell for eternity, you can avoid these coming horrors. Look at the futures of Cain, the millions prior to the flood, the evil kings of the Old Testament, and idol worshipers. The same fate will be shared by the Roman Empire emperors and the Jewish leaders of the Sanhedrin. An eternity in hell is waiting for Hitler, Mussolini, Hirohito, Stalin, Mao Zedong, and many others. These people cannot change their future; you can. By a simple prayer, asking for forgiveness of sins and accepting Jesus as your Savior, you will guarantee your future in heaven for eternity. Just be sure that your prayer is sincere.

The pastor who officiated my wedding to my wife would challenge the congregation during a Sunday service. After reciting a prayer of salvation, he asked if anyone had prayed the prayer. If anyone held up their hand, he would ask that person to look at him. He then would ask them if they meant what they prayed. I challenge you in the same way: make sure your prayer is sincere because God will know.

23

A Fraction of Time II

Read Luke 16:19-31

The preceding chapters contained alarming accounts of the woes contained within the twenty-one judgments and their respective wraths from God for those left behind after the rapture. Reader, I want to revisit a previous chapter and why we all must be ready for that fraction of time that will occur in a blink.

The reading for this chapter is a parable told by Jesus to His disciples and the others, including some of His detractors, the Pharisees. Jesus used these parables, fictional stories based on biblical truths, to help His followers understand Jesus, God Almighty, and the coming end times.

I have a parable to share with you, one that I wrote myself. Before I do, I want to tell you about a thriving program called Scared Straight, which takes kids who are in trouble with the law and puts them through a jail experience. The police match up these teenage offenders with prisoners in jail, who have been screened for this program. The teenagers are locked into the same cell with these select prisoners and get a real reality check about the reality of jail. This program is for boys and girls, and I have heard the results are effective. In my parable, you will read of a similar experience, but in a much different setting. Using Halloween as the time setting, this parable fits right into this scary season.

The following story is my parable. I am writing this chapter just prior to Halloween of 2021, with the real scares surrounding the coronavirus, very high crimes within the cities and towns, and threats of wars in several parts of the world. Here goes.

The youth pastor of the church had been speaking about the seven churches in the beginning chapters of Revelation, and the reasons for God's feelings toward them—good, bad, or just so/so. To end the series, which would be around Halloween, he wanted to combine the monthly youth meeting with a party surrounding celebrating Halloween in a godly manner. He met with everyone involved with the youth ministry. They planned a costume party, room decorations, and decided on a guest speaker. After the final youth meeting, the group started decorating the room. They hung an enormous spider web with a huge stuffed black widow spider from the ceiling of the room.

The day of the party, the youth pastor dressed up as a monk, and his wife was Cinderella. The other volunteers dressed up in various costumes. Even the senior pastor dressed up as Moses. The youth pastor encouraged the kids to bring an unsaved friend who did not attend church. Everything was ready, the food treats were made and ready to be served, and now they waited for the kids to arrive. Just before the doors opened, everyone gathered and offered a prayer for the evening.

The kids came rolling in wearing just about every kind of costume imaginable. A football player wore his football jersey and pads. A girl and her friend wore their cheerleader uniforms. Even Darth Vader from the Star Wars movies, light saber and all, showed up to the party. Laughter, scary stories, and practical jokes went flying throughout the room. And of course, the kids ate just about everything in sight. Even the senior pastor was laughing with all his might, watching the kids having such a good time.

One person nobody could recognize was someone dressed up in army camouflage, with his face painted in camouflage colors as well. He turned out to be the guest speaker the youth pastor had invited to speak that night. In fact, his costume was voted the best of the night; his prize was the first piece of the big cake made for the occasion.

After all the laughing, eating, and joking around, the youth pastor had everyone gather for the meeting of the night. He and the guest speaker, along with other volunteers, had made advanced plans for the night that would be part of the speaker's message to the kids. The first mystery was why two candles were at the front but were not lighted.

The youth pastor introduced the speaker and opened in prayer, as was his custom. Then the speaker read the verses from Luke 16 listed for this chapter. He began by covering what each character was in this life and where they ended up in the next. He explained that Hades, used in the verses, is another word for hell. Abraham's bosom was explained as a metaphor for heaven. He wanted the kids to understand exactly what Jesus was referring to when he talked about being in heaven or hell.

He addressed hell first, describing it as a place of unquenchable fire. He said the torment of those who are sent there never ends. Then he lighted the candles and told the kids that the flame is hell, which in Revelation is called a lake of fire. He told them that a better example would have been placing some kerosene in a punch bowl, then lighting the kerosene. He didn't demonstrate his example because he did not want to set off the fire sprinklers in the building.

Then the speaker compared the plight of the character Lazarus to where he was now in heaven. He cited some of the events of the day, their horrors, and even threats to the kids sitting in the room. He touched on some of the criminal acts, temptations to use drugs, and peer pressure to have sex before marriage.

He wasted no time telling the kids of just how real hell is and how all that they had been laughing and joking about that night was not funny at all. The kids were captivated by him as he described that when a person is burned beyond recognition, at some point that person does not feel the fire burning their body anymore. In hell, though, he said they will burn to the point of death but never stop feeling the extreme pain and pure agony.

The speaker then read the Bible description of the new heaven: its massive walls, the precious stones that comprise its foundation, and finally the twelve gates each containing a huge single pearl. Then he read from John 14 about Jesus preparing a mansion for each person who accepts Him as their Savior. He added verse 6, where Jesus said He is the only way of salvation. Pointing at the kids, he clarified that each person is responsible for where they will spend eternity.

The speaker then spoke about the day that is coming when Jesus will come for all who have accepted Him. Everyone who has not will be left behind to face an eternity in hell. He said not even Jesus knows when the day we call the rapture will occur as described in Matthew 24:36. Because of this fact, the speaker said, we must be ready now, as we may not have a then. A then may be the next minute, hour, day, year, or in a hundred years.

At this point, he asked the kids to do him a favor. "I want every one of you to bow your head, close your eyes, and please do not look or smile at each other," he said. "What I want you to concentrate on are the words I have to say."

After all of them had bowed their heads. The lights were turned off, so only the two candles burning could be seen.

The speaker paused for a moment, then in a deep voice, asked the kids where they would spend eternity if the rapture occurred at that moment. "You know that if it occurred right now," he said. "I would stop talking, maybe in the middle of a word. What would you do if I just stopped ta—"

He remained silent for a few moments, then one girl let out a bloodcurdling scream. "I do not want to go to hell!" Just then the lights were turned on and the speaker and the youth pastor's wife rushed to the girl. But she was not the only one in tears of fear.

Several of the kids who had been brought that night—some of whom had never been in church before—were in pure terror that the rapture had occurred, and they had been left behind.

Many kids had been scared into the loving arms of Jesus and a guarantee of an eternity in heaven. Later, when giving their public testimony of faith in Jesus at their baptismal service, many of them stated that if they had not been scared, they would never have given Jesus a passing thought. Today, many of those same kids are active in the church's youth ministry and have even found their spouses through that ministry.

Yes, this was a fictional story, but it's moral is oh so real!

You have read how my going blind and getting those documents from JH changed me and gave me a much clearer understanding of the coming end times. If you are reading this chapter, you can still make that life-changing decision to accept Jesus as your Savior.

Some of you may think that scaring people into receiving Jesus is not exactly the best idea. I beg to differ, because as I wrote in my parable, some of those kids would not have been saved had they not been scared into understanding the difference between heaven and hell.

In this short book, you have been given a layman's view and description of the coming events. Do not, I pray, allow yourself to be one of those who chooses to go another way besides Jesus, which leads to hell.

24

Witnessing to Others

Read Acts 1:1-11; 2:1-13

I trust and pray that when you read this chapter, I will be addressing all of you now as brothers and sisters in the Lord. I pray that through the witness of this book, you have accepted Jesus Christ as your Savior and Lord of your life. I know this for sure: you have read the way of salvation and will have no excuse should you be brought before the great white throne judgment.

With our salvation in Jesus, we also obtain a responsibility as witnesses for Jesus. In the reading for this chapter, we are recipients of what Jesus told His disciples on the Mount of Olives. This included what is called the great commission in Acts 1:8. First, Jesus said to remain in Jerusalem until the promised Holy Spirit has come, whom He referred to as the Comforter (John 14:26 KJV); Acts 1:4-5; 2:1-13).

Once the disciples received the Holy Spirit, among the miraculous things they were able to do included being able to speak in other languages. This is called "speaking in tongues" in the KJV. With this added talent, they could talk and witness to those from other areas who spoke different languages and were in Jerusalem for the feast. In doing so, the disciples fulfilled the first of the four-part commission from Jesus: being witnesses for Him in Jerusalem.

How do we today equate those places Jesus detailed to His disciples to locations where we can and should be witnesses for Him? The four places listed by Jesus were Jerusalem, Judea, Samaria, and the ends of the Earth. Let's look at these locations, as far as the disciples understood, and how they apply to us today.

When Jesus was on Earth, Jerusalem was the center of all things Jewish. It was the temple's location, where all the feasts described in the Mosaic Law (Exodus through Deuteronomy) should be held. It was a provincial capital of the ruling Roman Empire and was the location of both Jesus' crucifixion and resurrection. It was natural that the disciples should begin where they were in Jerusalem.

Where is our Jerusalem? As with the disciples, it is where we are now. Our next-door neighbors, the block or road we live on, and our city or county. We can even use our church building location as the point from which we branch out and witness for Jesus.

We must begin at home to secure a firm base of operations for witnessing. Before we start with even our neighbors, we need to begin our witness within the walls of our home with our family members. This should extend to family members who don't live with us, like brothers and sisters, in-laws, parents, and children of any age. Without a firm base of support and prayer supporters, we will probably have a stumbling start to our service for Jesus.

The example we have from Acts 2 is the disciples going out into the streets, gathering places, and the temple where they preached what Jesus had taught them. With the added talents given to them by the Holy Spirit, they were able to reach many for Jesus. Peter's preaching, recorded in this chapter, brought around three thousand into a saving knowledge of Jesus Christ.

Not all of us are like Billy Graham in our witnessing, reaching thousands. We can start with one family member, co-worker, or wayward teenager in the church to begin witnessing for Jesus. Some of us may not have the specific talent for sharing the Gospel, but we can be prayer warriors who support those who do. Also needed are people who can disciple new Christians, which involves increasing knowledge of God's Word and how to be future witnesses for Jesus. My manner of witnessing is writing books.

The next area was Judea, the Palestine region where Jerusalem was located. For us today, this might be the state or province where we live. In my case, I live in New Oxford, Pennsylvania. We could expand this to include the entire country.

Several years ago, our youth group from church traveled to Washington, D.C., a two-and-a-half-hour drive. We brought a bunch of Gospel tracts and spent part of our day handing out these tracts to those who were passing by our location. (Know that many cities today require permits to do this or hold any other kind of gathering, so make sure you comply with the ordinances before spreading the word about Jesus. You do not want to mess it up for others in the future.)

Try to orient your witness to the time of year and to those you will be contacting. If you are going to hand out tracts around Christmas, get tracts with that theme. Tracts have been written for witnessing to Jews that relate directly to their celebrations of Passover, Hanukah, Yom Kippur, etc.

Another thing you must be ready for in sharing Jesus is rejection. When we handed out tracts, some people would just throw them down on the sidewalk or road. The kids I was with that day did not allow that to deter them. They safely picked the tract back up, brushed it off, and handed to the next person. You want to keep a positive appearance and smile no matter what is said or done to you. Still, you do not have to tolerate any physical actions against you. In fact, I watched out for that while the kids handed out the tracts.

I suggest you practice dealing with all types of rejection at church, especially for any new Christians going out for the first time. Role-play some rejection scenarios, then discuss the best ways to respond to them. Some people can be rather cruel in rejecting you when you're witnessing for Jesus, so going out with some preparation is helpful.

The next area is Samaria, which in that day's Jewish world was a despised region of Palestine. Here's a little history to understand why this was the case.

When the Israelites first occupied the Promised Land in the book of Joshua, the tribe of Dan was given this area to live. However, this tribe is referred to as the lost tribe because they intermarried with the gentiles in that area, which God had strictly forbidden due to their idol worship. One example of idol worship was the Prophet Elijah, his meeting with the prophets of the idol Baal, and King Ahab and Queen Jezebel described in 1 and 2 Kings. So, the Jews did not have a favorable view of those who lived in Samaria.

In today's world, Samaria may be inner-city New York, Chicago, or any big city's internal streets. Dave Wilkerson's preaching on the streets of New York City led to the conversion of gang member Nikki Cruz. The story was later made into a movie called *The Cross and the Switchblade.* Our church has sent members to inner-city Chicago to conduct Vacation

Bible School for kids there and had positive results with the kids and parents. As I write this paragraph, seventeen missionaries are being held captive in Haiti for ransom by a very dangerous gang who has killed their captives in the past for failure to fulfill their demands.

Bringing a witness for Jesus to a modern-day Samaria may involve going to an area of the world to people who are not the nicest folks. The danger factor may be high, and the living conditions may be less than ideal. Anything associated with the Bible, Jesus, and Christianity is viewed rather severely by the locals and maybe even the government of that area.

This brings us to the final area Jesus referred to as the "ends of the Earth." Except for Antarctica, all the lands of the world are populated. Jesus meant that He died on the cross for all the sins of the world—for every person who lived, was living, and would live. Jesus wanted everyone to know what He had done for them and what His resurrection from the dead offered them.

The known world at the time Jesus spoke His words to the disciples was only about a quarter of what we know today. Even Paul's missionary travels covered just a portion of the eastern part of the Roman Empire. The disciples, and those after them, branched out into areas where little was known of the people and land; however, they were obedient to their commission from Jesus.

I remember an illustration from many years ago of how we could reach the entire world for Jesus. It was presented at our church while I was still living in Texas. The speaker held up a checkerboard with its sixty-four squares. Then he placed a single grain of rice on the first square. On the next square, he placed two grains of rice and kept doubling the number with each square.

He explained that the first grain represented a single witness for Jesus. That person leads another to Christ, making two witnesses for Jesus, and so on. He said that by the time you get to square sixty-four, there would be enough grains of rice to bury India fifty feet deep. In fact, you would pass a million and be only about one-third of the way through the checkerboard. Suppose we witnessed to just one person, and they accepted Jesus as their Savior. In that case, we can double the number of the redeemed in heaven. Then if all of us do it again, you get the point. But it starts with each of us obeying Jesus' commission in Acts 1:8. Will we always be successful? No, but we must never give up. Invite your neighbors to a special event at church, take them to a Christmas show where the message of salvation is presented, or just spend some one-on-one time with someone you know who does not know Jesus as Savior. It starts with one, so begin today.

Start your journey as a witness for Jesus by joining a new believer's class at your local Bible church. Nobody expects you to be ready to witness the next day. You must first grow in your own Christian maturity so when the world rejects you and your message at times, you can deal with such reactions and continue in your service for our Savior.

25

Now, Not Then

I cannot number the times I have been riveted by a movie or television show. Then the end comes with no definitive close, and I am left wondering what the ending or resolution to the subject will be. My wife and I had this reaction many times when watching the 1980s television show *Miami Vice*. Just when things were getting tight, the credits for who produced the show would come on the screen, and that was it. "Oh no!" we would holler, but that is how they ran that show. Thankfully, that is not how God directed His Bible to be written.

Throughout the Old and New Testaments, we are repeatedly told of God's wrath against sin and worshiping other gods than Him. In the first commandment, he says He is a jealous God. While Jesus was here on Earth, He stated many times we should serve His Father in heaven. This message really got under the skin of the Jewish leaders because Jesus claimed to be the Son of God, their Messiah. What they wanted in a Messiah was more like a general, not a Savior.

They felt this way because they were the enforcers of adherence to the Mosaic law, the requirements, and those restrictions they felt needed to be created to ensure the people obeyed the law. But Jesus rained on their parade. They desired to be revered by the people, and Jesus and His disciples did not follow the law in the ultra-strict manner they demanded.

Jesus saw right through these leaders and the sin they had

in their lives. He was also aware of their ignorance of the law as directed in the books Moses wrote. God was the only one who deserved their reverence; however, the Jewish leaders walked around as if the people should give their worship to them. Therefore, Jesus horribly irritated these men. Asking Jesus what the greatest commandment was demonstrated this magisterial view the Sanhedrin had of themselves (Matthew 22:36-40). Even the Old Testament prophets declared the sinful actions of this leadership. An example is when the prophet Malachi told the people that God would no longer accept their sacrifices because they offered less than acceptable animals to Him (Malachi 1:6-14).

I could list a page full of Bible references where God brought destruction to nations because of their worship of other gods. Even the Israelites did not get this message when they entered the promised land. Once sin came into the world, God showed His hatred of it with the flood, plagues on the Egyptians, and Israel's numerous defeats because of their idol worship. The prophets warned them, but like disobedient children, He had to teach them a lesson.

These past lessons by God on Israel were the background of Jesus' words in Matthew chapter 24. He wanted the disciples and us today to be warned of the coming final judgment against sin. Yes, Jesus paid the price for all our sins and conquered death. Without accepting Him as Savior, however, God would teach a lesson that will result in eternal punishment. Jesus, the Gospel writers, and others like Paul wanted us to know that now is the time to accept Jesus.

Many stories of tragedy came out in the past, from youth taking hallucinogenic drugs like lysergic acid diethylamide, better known by its acronym LSD. Then they would play the deadly "game" called Russian Roulette. A gun would have only one bullet in the chamber, then each player would spin the chamber, place the barrel to their head and pull the trigger. Once the gun went off, game over.

Those who decide to wait before becoming a Christian because they want to live a little are playing this same game. The difference is that the gun has a bullet in all the chambers. We have no idea when God the Father will decide to execute the rapture. Those who wait so they can "live it up" with sinful desires are plainly taking a fatal chance with their eternal existence.

Now is the time to accept Jesus as your Savior because you may not have a then!

26

Before the Blink

Throughout this book, I have been hammering those who are not saved to do so before that blink in time, the rapture. However, we who are Christians have a great responsibility here as well. In addition to being witnesses to the lost, we need to live like the Christians we claim to be in the presence of others.

Nothing is more hypocritical than going to church on Sunday, singing the hymns, and taking in the pastor's message, then the rest of the week, acting as a member of Satan's demonic choir by doing anything but living a life honoring our God.

Just because we have accepted Jesus as Savior does not mean we will not sin. In my case, I accepted Jesus as Savior at a church camp in Texas in 1966. In my late teens and twenties, however, I did anything but honor God, despite traveling to Israel on tours twice during this time. It finally took God flattening me with the loss of sight to reel me in and put me on a God-honoring road in His service. Since that time, I served as a civilian employee of the U.S. Army for twenty-seven years and eight months as a visually handicapped employee. I have also published six books and written two more.

First John 1:9 says all we need to do is confess our sins and God will forgive us. Until that day when we are called home, be it by death or rapture, we cannot escape the sin nature all of us were born with since the time of Adam and Eve. But we can and should strive to live as the Christians we claim to be before God and before those we desire to accept Jesus as Savior.

It pains me in many ways that when I was less than the Christian I should have been, how many people I may have turned away from Jesus because of my actions and reactions in front of others. I am sure you can think of times you wish you would have said or done something differently.

These less than good times will be the hay, wood, and stubble that will be burned away when we stand before the judgment seat of Christ in heaven. However, the upside is that we have a Savior who paid the price for all our sins before and after our salvation. All I know to say about that is "Praise the Lord!"

As we bring this book to a close, each of us needs to sit down and think of how we can tell others about Jesus, even those we may have acted like anything but a Christian in front of or around them.

We must remember that God isn't the only one who watches what we say and do. People we live with, our co-workers, and people we meet or see in the stores, restaurants, and even in church notice what we do.

There are many ways to witness to others as well. As I stated before, not all of us are or ever will be like the evangelist Billy Graham. But we can work in the hospitality area, teach a Sunday School class, serve in the nursery or children's rooms, youth or college ministries, or serve in an administrative office. You may even be called to serve God in a church pulpit or as a missionary in a foreign country. Due to our current times, in my church, unfortunately, we need people to serve as security officers for the church.

Any work done to glorify our God honors Him. Maybe you are good at maintenance, so you can mow the lawn around the church and keep things in repair. Most churches today have media functions, including audio and video during services and online. Wherever the talents God gave you fit into the church and the witness it brings to the community, do that activity to the best of your ability. This service is crucial to reaching the goal of bringing others into a saving knowledge of Jesus Christ.

God wants all to spend eternity in heaven, and we should keep that thought in mind because we are only a blink away from that day God calls His own to heaven. I ask you, Will I see you there? That should also be our desire for everyone we meet in this life. Be ready to witness because that is our commission until we are gone in a blink.

References

If you have decided to accept Jesus Christ as your Savior, or maybe you rededicated your life to follow Him, well done! I urge you to contact a pastor at a Bible church near you. Also, contact one of the following:

The Billy Graham Evangelistic Association at
www.bgea.org

Intouch Ministries of Dr. Charles Stanley at
www.intouch.org

Turning Point of Dr. David Jeremiah at
www.davidjeremiah.org

About the Author

KEVIN TURNBAUGH was born on August 10, 1954 in Bad Axe, Michigan, and graduated from Hanover High School, Hanover, PA, in 1972. He was employed for a short time in the meat packing industry, then for thirteen years in the shoe industry as an industrial engineer. For the next twenty-seven plus years, he served as a General Supply Specialist civilian employee for the U.S. Army.

During an eye examination in 1984, he was diagnosed with the eye disease Retinitis Pigmentosa (RP), and in 1999, he went totally blind. He is the author of five previous books, and his website is: https://www.timewitnessing.com. All of his books were written on a computer equipped with a speech software that allows him to hear what is being typed. It is this same software that assisted him throughout most of his career with the Army, where he received several performance awards from the Commanding General.

In January 2019, Kevin suffered a small stroke, that affected his speech and ability to walk without the assistance of a walker. However, he does not intend to allow this added handicap to keep him from forwarding the Gospel to others through his books or in his limited public speaking events.

.

CPSIA information can be obtained
at www.ICGtesting.com
Printed in the USA
BVHW090457270922
647999BV00005B/15

9 781956 365313